MAKE MONEY WITH YOUR PC!

THE REVISED GUIDE TO STARTING AND RUNNING SUCCESSFUL BUSINESSES WITH YOUR PERSONAL COMPUTER

••••••••••••••••••
LYNN WALFORD

TEN SPEED PRESS
BERKELEY, CALIFORNIA

Copyright © 1994 by Lynn Walford. All rights reserved. No part of this book may be reproduced or transmitted in any form or by any means, electronic or mechanical, including photocopying and recording, or by any information storage and retrieval system, without written permission from the author, except for the inclusion of brief quotations in a review.

Revised Edition

Cover design by Ten Arts Services, Culver City, California
Text design by Toni Tajima

Library of Congress Cataloging-in-Publication Data

Walford, Lynn.
   Make money with your PC! : a guide to starting and running successful PC-based businesses / Lynn Walford. -- Rev. ed.
     p. cm.
   Includes bibliographical references and index.
   ISBN 0-89815-606-8 : $7.95
     1. Home-based businesses -- Managment.   2. New business enterprises -- Management.   3. Microcomputers.   I. Title
HD2333.W34   1994
658'.041--dc20   94–29
                                                                              CIP

Trademarked names appear throughout this publication. Rather than provide a list of trademark holders, or use trademark symbols to denote trademarked names, the publisher and author acknowledge the trademarks and are using them for editorial purposes only. No intention has been made to use any of these names generically. Readers are cautioned to investigate a claimed trademark before using it for any purpose other than referring to the product to which it is attached.

Printed in the United States of America.
1 2 3 4 5 — 98 97 96 95 94

ACKNOWLEDGMENTS

I am honored to have the privilege of working with an excellent publishing company, Ten Speed Press. The creative vision and unique sense of humor of editor in chief George Young have been an inspiration to me. Associate editor Alexis Brunner has been a delight to work with and has helped me laugh through my mistakes.

I am grateful for many people in my life who do not realize how much their being around nurtures my abilities and contributes to my life: Becky Loving, Arthur Mortimer, and Becky Thaler.

I am also indebted to organizations where I have learned everything I needed exactly when I needed it: The Independent Writers of Southern California, The Los Angeles Computer Society, The Book Publicists of Southern California and COSMEP.

Over the years dealing with PCs, I have always found a helpful hand and sage advice from Jilbert Sinehi at Central Technology.

I could not have written this book without new innovative technology from companies that truly care about the health of PC users: The Kinesis Corporation, Ergodyne, MicroCentre, and Quill Corporation.

Steve and Lisa Carlson at Upper Access Books, world-renowned book publicist Irwin Zucker, and Dean Guiliotis all contributed to the selling and making of *Make Money with Your PC!* They filled my work with joy, laughter, and knowledge.

I am grateful to Bruce Johnson, senior instructor at The Westside Center for Independent Living, who helped me find wonderful resources for the disabled.

I recognize the great amount of support my mother, Elaine, and my sister, Diane, have given me throughout my life.

I also thank the thousands of students who have told me exactly what they wanted in a book, laughed at my jokes, confided in me, and enriched my life with their experiences.

DISCLAIMER

This book is designed to provide information pertinent to the subject matter covered. It is sold with the understanding that the publisher and author are not engaged in rendering legal, accounting, or other professional services. If legal or other expert assistance is required, the services of a competent professional should be sought.

PC-based businesses are not get-rich-quick schemes. Anyone starting a PC-based business must expect to invest time and effort. Every effort has been made to make this publication as accurate as possible. Effort has also been made to supply the most current information regarding software publishers and products discussed in this book. However, Ten Speed Press assumes no responsibility for any infringements of patents or other rights of third parties which would result.

This text should be used only as a general guide and not as the ultimate source of PC-based business information. Since computer information changes daily it is good practice to check with the most up-to-date periodical before you make any computer software or hardware buying decision.

The purpose of this book it to educate and entertain. The author and Ten Speed Press shall have neither liability nor responsibility to any person or entity with respect to any consequential loss or other damages caused or alleged to be caused directly or indirectly by the information contained in this book.

POLITICALLY CORRECT PC USAGE?

NOTE: For the purposes of this book a PC is defined as any personal computer, including Macintosh, even though PC is often used for IBM-compatible personal computers. When writing about software and hardware, I had to limit the book to IBM-compatible and Mac because they have the largest market share. It doesn't mean, however, that you cannot use the principles and exercises in this book to make money with your Amiga, CPM, Unix, or computer of your own design. In fact, this book could be used for starting any business.

Table of Contents

Introduction 1

1 Let's Get Started! 5
   Do You Really Want to Start a Computer-Based Business 5
   Chapter 1 Exercises 9

2 The Perfect Match 11
   How to Choose the Right Computer-Based Business 11
   Computer-Based Business Success Stories 11
   Finding Your Market 13
   How to Create a Computer-Based Business Idea 14
   Skill Power 15
   Business Classifications 15
   Chapter 2 Exercises 22

3 Taking the First Steps: Setting Up Your Business 23
   Ready Set Go! 23
   Chapter 3 Exercises 29
   Checklist of First Steps 30

4 Software Awareness 31
   The Determinator 31
   Choosing the Right Software for You 31
   General Types of Software Packages 33
   Chapter 4 Exercises 47
   Software Reminders 48

5 Hardware Made Easy 49
   Meet Your New Best Friend, Your Computer 49

Chapter 5 Exercises 67
Hardware Reminders 68

6 PAIN IN THE NECK AVOIDANCE..69
Only You Can Prevent Computer-Related Pain........................69
Chapter 6 Exercises 77

7 PLANNING YOUR BUSINESS 79
Your Map to Success 79
Chapter 7 Exercises 83
Checklist for Business Planning 84

8 MARKETING YOUR BUSINESS...85
Tools of the Marketing Trade...85
Chapter 8 Exercises 101

9 MANAGING YOUR BUSINESS..103
Managing It All..103
Chapter 9 Exercises 109

10 LET'S GET BUSY! 111
Making the Transition 111
Create Your Own Exercises..114

RESOURCE GUIDE 115

INTRODUCTION

As prices of personal computers reach an all-time low and software automates complicated tasks, it is becoming easier to run a profitable business from your computer, either full- or part-time. Throughout the country, entrepreneurs are using computers to service the needs of many industries. Computer-based businesses are a major part of the growing force of home-based businesses. In 1995 BIS Strategic Decisions estimates that about 43% of U.S. households will have some form of home office, with 24.7 million income-producing offices and 6.3 million telecommuters! New affordable technology, downsizing and outsourcing of big business, environmental concerns, and the desire of workers to create their own jobs are all contributing to this growth.

But where do you go to find out about an industry this new? Through researching my own business and the classes I teach, I have found many useful sources, trade secrets, and good business rules that apply to all computer-based companies, as well as many unique ideas that may give you the skills to become successful. This information is too valuable to keep to myself, which is why I wrote *Make Money with Your PC!*

I have researched this subject extensively, but also learned the hard way—through experience. I have included my own story and those of my students, friends, and colleagues to show you how to avoid making the same mistakes we all did—mistakes which could have been prevented if we had known where to go for information and help.

This book is designed for those of you who want to make extra money in your spare time with your personal computer; those currently in the business world planning to start your own business;

1

or those who have started your own business and want to find ways to make it more successful. All it really takes to be successful is a minimal investment, an understanding of your natural strengths, research, perseverance, and good business sense.

In this book you will find out:

> *If starting your own computer-based business is right for you.*
> *How to determine the right business for your skills.*
> *How to evaluate and choose hardware and software.*
> *Several proven successful business ideas.*
> *How to market and manage your business.*
> *How to price, bill, and get paid for your services.*
> *How to set up your business.*
> *Where to go for help.*

Since starting your own business takes a lot of discipline, I have created exercises at the end of each chapter as your homework. Although you will not be graded, the rewards for doing a good and thorough job are great. After all, whatever you put into your business will always come back to you. Brainstorming ideas are also included for you to inspire sessions with friends, colleagues, or family members and stimulate new and exciting ideas.

This book is laid out in a natural step-by-step process, but feel free to skip around and move in the sequence that works best for you. I suggest that you use a loose-leaf binder and keep track of all your exercises and planning in it. Your efforts will be more productive if you can find your notes easily. I also suggest that you don't make any major buying decisions until after you have read the entire book and completed all the exercises.

If you find this book valuable, please tell your friends, and let

INTRODUCTION

me know how your business is doing. Since I teach "Make Money with Your PC!" classes at colleges, I love success stories to share with my students. You can write to me c/o Ten Speed Press, P.O. Box 7123, Berkeley, CA 94707.

May you make more money with your computer than you ever dreamed possible.

Best wishes,

Lynn Walford

1 ♦ LET'S GET STARTED!

DO YOU REALLY WANT TO START A COMPUTER-BASED BUSINESS?

HOW DO YOU SPELL SUCCESS?

I start off every one of my "Make Money with Your PC!" classes by asking my students the question, "How do you define success?" Everyone has a different answer: "Obtaining my goals." "Being able to make my own hours." "Having time to travel or be with my kids." "Being able to work at home." And, always, "Making money doing something that I enjoy doing."

Before you decide to start any business, it is important to think about how you define success. Some of you may just want to make enough money to pay for your computer, others may dream of massive wealth. Whatever success means to you, when you know what kind of success you want, you can decide the most profitable and rewarding way to achieve it.

Many people have reached their own special kind of success with the use of personal computers. Entrepreneurs like Bill Gates at Microsoft and Terrese Meyers, cofounder of Quarterdeck Office Systems, both started working out of garages to become CEOs of multimillion-dollar companies. Former welfare participants and physically disabled people have found ways to make money that enhance their lives and the lives of others with personal computers. Homemakers are able to take care of their homes and children while creating computer-based businesses that allow them the time to have a career and a family. Senior citizens enhance their retirement income with their computers for fuller enjoyment of their golden years. A variety of different kinds of people have been successful with their computers because there are a variety of different businesses you can start with a personal computer.

Most computer-based businesses provide services. You sell these services to people who need them and then they pay you for your work and output. For instance, your computer can do accounting, design T-shirts, keep track of thousands of addresses, create beautiful wedding programs, and connect up to information in online services which you can repackage and sell. It can even be programmed to remind you of your appointments or when to pay your bills. You can have a full-time staff with one computer for less than it would cost you to pay one month's salary of a good office manager.

Computer-based businesses have an added advantage over large megacorporations which can't meet the needs of our changing markets; computer-bizers who are not saddled with vast corporate infrastructure can make changes almost instantly! When you own your own business, you can set your own hours, and when you find a faster, easier way of doing something you can increase your income and the money in your pocketbook.

Most people start their own business because they want to be their own boss and want a sense of independence. For instance, I work anywhere from 18 to 90 hours a week. There are days when I have sat in front of the computer screen until 2:00 A.M. Other days, I work only a few hours and spend most of the day shopping and at the gym. Never being happy in a regular job, I was almost forced to start my own business. I used to beat myself up because I couldn't last in jobs and became bored instantly. Now I find that I am never bored with my work because I created a business to accommodate my own needs for success and happiness.

If anyone were to look at my employment history they would never consider hiring me. I have a degree from Pomona College in Theater Arts. I have worked as a theatrical stage manager, a theater publicist, and a catering cook/waitress/food designer. I taught kindergarten and first grade, sold designer sportswear, sold radio time and wrote radio commercials, and have performed stand-up comedy. I have been a word processor, legal secretary, and finally a desktop publisher. Many of the jobs were part-time and done simultaneously. In each of my jobs, I picked up skills that I now use in my own business.

All of your jobs, whatever your role—a volunteer, parent, or tightrope walker—have given you unique skills that you can turn into a profitable business. Your abilities teamed with a computer will save you time and make you money.

Since computer-based businesses are fairly inexpensive to start, you can buy and own the same equipment that the big guys use and still not need to take out a second mortgage to buy them. You can easily start part-time while you are working at another job. When I started freelancing as a computer trainer and desktop publisher, I worked part-time for another desktop publisher. What was great about the job was that it was flexible and I learned from someone else's mistakes while I still was able to pay the bills. Once you decide what type of business or service you want to start, you can find a part-time or freelance job working for someone else in that business, where you earn while you learn.

Sound too good to be true? There are some problems to overcome. That's why planning is so important. Don't quit your job until you know that you will be able to make enough money to live off. It does take time and effort to develop clients and you won't get them instantly. You have to provide your own health insurance and there is no unemployment insurance. If you make enough, it's worth paying for your own insurance. Some cities have laws that limit your ability to expand. By planning, and by contacting your city, state, and county, you can find out any limitations before you start.

U.S. tax laws are set up to encourage business. Once you become self-employed, you can take many deductions that an employee cannot—before you even pay your taxes. You will need to learn about the laws, but anyone who can use a phone and read can find out all the information needed from the IRS. The IRS wants you to prosper: the more money you make, the more money the government makes from you. The most important part of planning your business is knowing how much money you need to pay out for your expenses and how much money you need to bring in in order for you to be successful and happy.

••••••••••••••••••••••

Now that you're seriously thinking about starting a computer-based business, what's next? Complete the exercises at the end of this chapter, then decide what type of business you will be the best at with the help provided in Chapter 2.

📖 LET'S GET STARTED!

✍ CHAPTER 1 EXERCISES

Write your answers in your binder.

1. How do you define success?
    a. What does it feel and look like?
    b. Do you believe that your kind of success is possible? If not, why?
    c. How can you make success possible?
2. Why do you want to start your own business?
3. Do you truly believe that you can work on your own and be disciplined?
4. How much money do you need to make to meet your expenses and make you happy?
5. What types of activities do you excel at? People-related? Number-related? Detail-oriented?
6. Are you an expert in any field? Do you have a special talent that people are always amazed at?
5. How much money do you think it will take to start your business? (Guess for now. You will do more detailed calculations later.)
6. What do you need to do to be closer to finding the kind of business you want?
    a. Is there a way you can find out what you need in the next week? If so, set a time to do it.
7. Make a list of the advantages and disadvantages of starting your own business.

    How could you improve your chances of succeeding?
8. What would be the absolute worst thing that could happen in starting a business?
    a. How could you prevent it?

When you are finished and sure you want to start your own computer-based business, start reading Chapter 2.

9

2 ♦ THE PERFECT MATCH

HOW TO CHOOSE THE RIGHT COMPUTER-BASED BUSINESS

There are literally hundreds of businesses you can start with your computer. You need to choose which one will be the most successful for you. Through the years of studying computer-based businesses, I have found that most successful computer-based businesses have had one or more of the following factors in common:

1. The business started with a good idea.
2. The business was based on the owner's natural talents and skills and required work that the owner enjoyed doing.
3. The business fulfilled a demand/need for the service. (If that business was the first to fulfill that demand/need, its profitability increased.)
4. The business used commercially available software packages, or programmed packages to do specialized functions.

COMPUTER-BASED BUSINESS SUCCESS STORIES

BILLS THAT PAY

Bill, a student in one of my classes, shared how he started his very profitable bill-paying business. He was working on film sets in Hollywood, where 12-hour days are considered short. The crew often worked from 6:00 A.M. to 9:00 P.M., leaving them little time to do anything but work—including paying their bills. When Bill overheard someone talking on the set about how she hated to sit down and write out checks because she never had time, he saw a money-making opportunity, and seized it. He bought an inexpensive accounting program and began selling his bill-paying service.

Bill knew the movie business and he tailored his business to meet the specific needs of those working in the industry. Because he used a computer, he could automate the writing and printing of checks, which was something his clients couldn't do. Within a few months, he no longer had to work long hours on movies sets to make money and more than paid his bills by paying other people's bills. He hired other people to do most of the work and went to the beach when he felt like it.

There are numerous accounting programs that lend themselves to starting a bill-paying business. On the other hand, there are billing businesses. For example, a growing field right now is Medical Billing, because there are so many different forms and ways of billing for insurance and Medicare. There are specific programs for doctors, dentists, and chiropractors. Do you have a background in some field that uses a bill-paying or billing service?

YOUR CHECK'S IN THE MAIL

Henry also worked in the movie industry. As a gofer, he saw that distribution companies often sent personally addressed letters to clients and vendors. However, because the distributors did not back up their data, they did not keep track of their correspondence and often lost records. Henry knew he could figure out a better system which would not only save the distributors money, but make him money as well. Today, the studios pay him on a regular basis to write personalized letters and keep databases of their correspondence.

Many businesses need information from databases. Database programs can be programmed to do all sorts of tricks. For instance, accounting reports that used to take a week to generate have been automated in Paradox, and now only take a few minutes. This kind of automation can translate into a great business idea. What kinds of businesses need these kinds of programs? You could start a specialized database service for those businesses and increase their productivity—and your income!

GRAPHICAL USERS INTERFACE WITH PROFIT

Dean Guiliotis always drew, painted, and sketched for fun. When he saw how easy it was to create designs on the computer, he saw a great income opportunity. Now Dean, "The Design Machine," works over 70 hours a week designing corporate logos, and a variety of other graphic work. He uses Aldus Freehand and other desktop publishing/page layout and photograph manipulation programs. He finds that most of his customers are new businesses and specialty advertising companies (companies that imprint logos on key chains, mugs, T-shirts, etc.).

"I find my work more rewarding than any job that I have ever had, and I have a potential to make more money!" says Guiliotis, who is "living very comfortably after only a year in business." He does advise, however, "The computer and programs are just tools. You have to have a talent to use them successfully."

COMPUTER CONSULTING

By 1995, 90% of all businesses will be using computers, and these businesses will need help with the selection and setup of their systems. I have found in my computer consulting practice that businesses are willing to pay well for someone who can explain complicated computer hardware/software jargon in plain English. Small to mid-size businesses which can't afford a full-time consultant love the fact that I am on call and available to them when they need me. My specialties are training and setting up desktop publishing programs. I have always enjoyed communicating with people and also have a knack for figuring out very complex puzzles (which is what installing software and computer equipment is like—a complex puzzle.)

FINDING YOUR MARKET

Most successful computer-based businesses have found a market with a need that matched the talents and abilities of their owners. Spend time researching your business and your potential clientele.

The library is a great source of information. You should also read your local paper to find out where there may be a market specific to your area that has not been covered. Join associations and community groups and ask and listen to find out what is going on in your area.

A good way to research your business is by using your telephone. Phone several potential clients and ask quickly and nicely, "Do you ever have a need for___?" Most people will tell you the truth. You could even use the old student disguise and say "I'm researching a project at ___ College and was wondering, do you have a need for___?" The more information you have about your potential clients, the better.

You should also research your future business competition. Are they really servicing the needs of the community? Are they open during convenient hours? Are they easy to get to? How could you make that business better?

How to Create a Computer-Based Business Idea

June Christopher wished that there was a service that would enter old scripts into computer file format, and figured that others also might need this service. She bought a scanner and some OCR (Optical Character Recognition) software and now has a long customer waiting list.

If you wished that a specific kind of software program existed, it probably does—and maybe no one has thought of starting a business with it. To find out about various programs, read computer software magazines, join User Groups where you can network with other computer users, and check references. There may be a business you can create that makes people's wishes come true. What kind of services do you, your friends, and your businesses associates wish for?

SKILL POWER

Most people have the skills and abilities to do all the work necessary in order to succeed. Sometimes, we don't realize that we have the capabilities that we do. A student of mine named Agnes once proclaimed, "I don't have any salable skills. All I have ever done is work for the IRS for over 30 years!" I then asked the class, "How many people would want Agnes to prepare your taxes?" Everyone in the class raised their hands. Agnes had not seen how valuable her skills were.

Most skills can be very valuable when they are used to fulfill a need. To find out the types of businesses which match your skills, read the following lists carefully and see what appeals to you. Which business best suits your skills? What new business idea can you create with your skills? (Remember, you can combine several different business ideas to create a new one of your own.)

BUSINESS CLASSIFICATIONS

The general categories for computer-based businesses are:

Accounting & Number-Related—businesses that use accounting software, spreadsheets, and mathematical functions.

Art & Publishing-Related—businesses that require a good eye and maybe a little artistic ability.

Computer-Related—businesses that require analytical and technical skills, as well as a good understanding of how computers work.

Database-Related—businesses that require searching, retrieving, formatting, or analyzing information.

Word Processing Related—these businesses are based on word input and output. Some require good writing and grammar skills.

Miscellaneous and Multifaceted—these businesses may use one or many programs and talents.

ACCOUNTING & NUMBER-RELATED BUSINESSES

Mortgage broker Diane Rodgers figured she could use a loan program and her computer to help people get the best mortgage rates around when she couldn't find a qualified loan agent. She figured right and ended up with a successful refinancing business.

In which of the following businesses can you turn your numerical ability into profitability?

Abstracting Service

Accountant

Actuary

Auditor

Bill-Paying Service

Budget Analyst

Collection Service

Economist

Financial Planner

Golf Handicapping

Medical Billing

Mortgage Auditor/Broker

Payroll Service

Professional Time and Billing Service

Property Management

Sales Analysis

Sports League Statistics

Statistical Analysis

Stock and Financial Analyst

Tax Preparation

ART & PUBLISHING-RELATED BUSINESSES

When Anne, a former student of mine, was a secretary, she learned a great deal about presentation graphics. She took what she had learned, started a presentation graphics business with her computer, ended up making more money than she had in her previous job, *and* was able to set her own hours!

How can your graphic and artistic abilities draw money and success into your life through one of the following businesses?

Advertising Design

Animation

Annual Report Design

Astrology and Numerology

Biorhythm Forecasts

Book Publishing

■ THE PERFECT MATCH

- Book Design
- Brochure Design
- Business Cards and Stationery Design
- Business Plan Design
- Business Proposals
- Catalogues (typesetting or design)
- Computer Art
- Computer Portraits
- Computer-Aided Cartooning
- Computer-Aided Design
- Computer and Electronic Documentation
- Coupon Books
- Desktop Multimedia (text, graphics, sound)
- Desktop Publishing
- Desktop Video
- Directory Publishing
- Direct-Mail: Writing, Design, or Mailing
- DTP Service Bureau
- Financial Report Design
- Form Design
- Free Classified Advertising Newspaper
- Graphics (for transfer to videotape or film)
- Greeting Card Design
- Guide Publishing (shopping, city, bargains)
- Magazine Publishing, Design, or Typography
- Menu Typography (especially good for restaurants with daily specials or changing menus)
- Multimedia Presentations
- Newsletter Design
- Organization and Flow Chart Services
- Package Design
- Personalized Christmas Cards, Children's Books, etc.
- Presentation Graphics
- Presentation Graphics for Slides and Overheads
- Promotional Materials
- Repair Manuals (car and any other industry)
- Resume Service
- Sign-Making Service
- Specialized T-shirts, Mugs, Caps: Design or Manufacturing
- Technical Manual (writing and design)
- Technical Books (writing and design)

Tests (publishing)

Ticket and Program Design

Training Manuals and Materials (writing and design)

Typesetting or graphics (signs, labels, maps, etc.)

Typesetting (Journals, Medical Journals, Literary Journals)

COMPUTER-RELATED BUSINESSES

Mike Simmons started his online bulletin board service when he was eleven years old because it was "fun." Now at sixteen, Mike has his own office in Palm Springs, over 4,000 subscribers to his service, and is planning to reach his goal of grossing over $1 million in a year, soon.

Which of the following computer-related businesses look like "fun" to you?

Bar Coding Service

Computer Rentals/ Service Bureau

Computer-based Game Development

Computer Embroidery

Computer Bulletin Board Service

Computer Consultant

Computer Programmer

Computer Repair

Computer Software Training

Data Conversion Service

Debugging Software

Disk Tutorials

Disk Storage, Disk Space/ Time Sharing

Disk Copying and Formatting Service

Electronic Voice Mail/ Answering Service

Fax on Demand Service

Scanning Service

Technographer

Used Computer Broker

Voice Mail Message Center

THE PERFECT MATCH

DATABASE-RELATED BUSINESSES

With Russia becoming a free economy, there has been an increase in research needs for new businesses. Kiril Tchascin, a market researcher from Moscow, has filled this need by using his modem and his notebook computer to access databases all over the world.

What kind of business can you start with your database resources?

Abstracter

Baby-sitting Referral Service

Buying or Pricing Service

Computer-Aided Telemarketing

Create and Manage Client Databases

Family History and Historical Name Analysis and Search

Electronic Clipping Service

Expert Locating Service (a.k.a. Expert Broker)

Fax Sending and Receiving

Government Bid Notification Service

Government Form Filling and Filing Service

Home Inventory Service

Household Service Referral Agency

Indexing

Information Broker

Inventory Control

Mail Order

Mailing Service/Mailing Labels

Market Study and Research

Matchmaker/Computer Dating

Nursing Registry for Patients

Pen Pal Service

Pollster

Public Opinion Service

Real Estate Listings

Records Management

Roommate Finding and Matching Service

Sale of Mailing Lists

Scholarship Search Service

Specialized Broker

Specialized Employment Agency

WORD PROCESSING-RELATED BUSINESSES

Flo Selfman really knows how to make the most of her writing abilities and her word processing software. Not only does she own a public relations firm, but she also provides editing and proofreading services, and leads seminars on the use of punctuation.

What kind of businesses can you start with your writing and word processing abilities?

Business Proposals

Copy Editor

Copywriter

Correspondent

Data Entry

Employee Manual Writing

Foreign Language Word Processing

Grammar Correction

Grant Writer

Legal Forms: Filing and Filling

Manuscript Critiques

Newsletter Writing

Paralegal Services

PR/Publicist

Technical and Scientific Word Processing

Technical Writer

Transcription (Medical, Legal, Insurance)

Transcribing (Radio and TV Programs)

Translation

Typing/Word Processing/Secretarial Service

Writer

MISCELLANEOUS AND MULTIFACETED BUSINESSES

Steve and Lisa Carlson wrote and published books with their computer. To help market their books, they started a catalog of various books from small presses. To keep track of inventory and sales, they created a database specifically designed for their small publishing business. Now they sell their software to publishers all over the world, including many of the publishers listed in the catalog. They created a multifaceted business with a unique combination of software programs.

THE PERFECT MATCH

How can you combine some of the following services to create your own multifaceted business?

Booking Agent

CD-ROM Reference

Contest Organizer

Cost Estimator

Educational Consultant

Employee Applications Checking Service

Event and Meeting Planner

Instructional Design

Interior Design, with Computer-Generated Previews

Music Publishing and Scoring with a Computer

Purchasing Agent

Reunion Planning

Specialized Research

Are there any other kinds of businesses you can think of to start? In this fast changing world there may be a new service that you can be the first to offer and therefore make the most profit at.

📖 CHAPTER 2 EXERCISES

1. Write down the businesses that you like the best.
2. Which of the businesses you have chosen seem to be the most interesting to you? The most exciting? Which look like fun and have the greatest potential for you to use your wonderful skills?
3. Next to each business you have chosen, write down the skills you already have that would help you in that business.
4. During the next week research the businesses you have chosen:
    a. Go to the library and look them up in periodicals and books.
    b. Look in the yellow pages for possible competition.
    c. Call similar businesses and ask questions about what they do and how much they charge.
    d. Are the businesses you visited missing an audience that you could reach more easily? Are they busy? Are they providing good customer service? How could you improve on their business?
5. The best way to follow market trends is to read the paper and keep your eyes, ears, and heart open. Read the papers and any pertinent publications that relate to your skills. Listen for requests: Has someone at work, at the hairdresser, gym, or garage said, "I wish there was a service that would...?"

Work through these exercises until you know which business is best for you. When you finally decide on your business, state precisely what type of business you are starting, the services you will provide, and who would benefit from your services. Be sure to write it all down.

3 ✦ TAKING THE FIRST STEPS: SETTING UP YOUR BUSINESS

Ready Set Go!

Once you know the kind of business you want to start, there will be many decisions you have to make. Starting any business is a process, and you will learn as you go along what the best way of doing things is for you. In this chapter we will look at all the major steps involved in starting and running a successful computer-based business. The chapters following this overview will walk you through these steps in greater detail.

✎ NOTE: I placed the steps of starting up a business in an order that seemed logical for most people. However, you may find that a different order or routine will work best for you. If that is the case, jumping around the chapter may make more sense for you than reading it straight through. You may even want to re-read certain sections at various stages of startup when you have a better understanding of what it is you're going to need to know to put together your business.

STEP ONE: WHERE DO YOU START?

If you are going to work with your computer, the first thing you will need to decide is where you are going to work with it. Are you going to rent an office or work at home?

Since a computer takes up a minimal amount of room, it may be easier for you to start working from your home. With the advent of fax machines, and modems, it is no longer necessary to contact clients in person. However, if you are in a hard-to-reach location and clients will be coming to see you personally, rather than you going to them, you may want to consider renting an office. However, using an office will cost more than working at home and may make it more difficult for you to meet your expenses.

For some businesses the extra expense is worth it. For instance, Key Ticklers is a word processing and typing service in an office building in Century City, filled with lawyers and professionals who need typing and word processing services. Most of their clients are in the building and are clients because of their convenient location. The extremely high rent they pay is worth it.

Your local government may require certain permits to work at home, or business licenses. If you are selling products, you may be required to charge sales tax. In some states, such as California, some types of desktop publishing output is taxable. Be sure to call the necessary offices to find out what the regulations are in your area for your service. If you are not sure what offices to call, ask your local chamber of commerce or librarian.

There are many positives and negatives to working at home. Your choice of workplace may depend on who you live with; some parents like to be near their children, while others like to work away from home. Decide what location will work best for you and your business by weighing the pros and cons of your various choices.

✏ **NOTE:** Your mother told you not to let strangers know where you live. Mom was right: You may run into weirdos in the course of business. If you are working from your home, using a mail box center or post office box as your business address could prevent major problems. (The post office will not accept UPS or delivery service packages; a mail box center will. Also, if you are running ads in newspapers in certain states you must have a business street address and therefore will need a mail box center.)

STEP TWO: BUSINESS PHONES

The first place many people look when they don't know how to find a skilled person is in the yellow pages. In order to be listed in the yellow pages, you will need a business phone. Business phones are more expensive than personal phones, so if you do put a busi-

▣ Taking the First Steps: Setting Up Your Business

ness phone into your home, you can accept incoming calls on it and use your home phone for outgoing calls. When you file your tax return you can claim all of your business phone bills as an expense, but only toll and long distance calls on your personal phone.

If you decide on a business phone, call the phone company immediately and find out when the deadline is for an ad in yellow pages. Be patient: It may be a year before anyone calls from your ad or listing.

STEP THREE: THE NAME GAME

Once you have decided on the business that you are going to start and where it will be, you need to decide what you will call your service. If you use your own name, you do not have to file a Fictitious Business Statement. (If you want to open a separate business account in your business name, most banks require a Fictitious Business Statement or D.B.A.) If you are doing all of the work yourself, and you have a strong background in your chosen business, you can use your name followed by a title, such as Fred Smith, Desktop Publisher, and name your company later.

How to Choose a Name

1. Make sure it is memorable.

2. The closer to the beginning of the alphabet the better for listing in directories. Zaba's Typing Service may be your dream name, but clients may never get to your name at the end of an alphabetical list.

3. Your name should promote a clear image of what your business does and who you are trying to reach. You don't want to outgrow your name. (In a class recently, a student told of a prominent caterer who started out her company with a name something like Municipal Food. The name of her company does not go well with the glamorous Hollywood Party Set and the owner has to work hard to maintain her sophisticated image.)

4. Check local yellow pages, industry directories, national phone directories (available on CD-ROM or via online services) and county D.B.A. filings to see if there are any other businesses with your name. Running a trademark search via online services will also ensure that no one else is using your name.

5. Test your name out with friends, relatives, and colleagues to see what their impressions of it are and what they perceive it to mean.

STEP FOUR: SETTING UP YOUR HARDWARE, SOFTWARE, AND WORK AREA

Since your business will be based around your computer, you will need to spend time deciding on the best software, hardware, and work area setup for you.

Choosing software, hardware, furniture, and other computer devices can be a very complicated task. Sometimes you may feel like you're going around in circles. Be patient and take your time. Read the chapters on the topics you need to know about, do the exercises, do your research, and use your best judgment.

STEP FIVE: LEARNING HOW TO USE YOUR EQUIPMENT

Now that you've got your new computer supertoy, how do you learn to use it? Hopefully you have already had some computer experience; if not, you can learn how to use it many ways:

1. Classes at adult schools and community colleges.

2. Tutorials that come with the programs themselves.

3. Video tapes that you buy or rent from video stores or libraries.

4. Third party books and manuals.

5. User groups.

6. Friends.

7. Online services.

▣ Taking the First Steps: Setting Up Your Business

When I first got my computer and I started reading the manuals, my eyes would cross and glaze over because I had no idea what they were talking about. I learned the hard way—on my own. Looking back, I wish I had taken a class because I would have learned a lot faster. Depending on your personal learning style, choose the best teaching method for you.

User Groups

A user group is a group of computer users who meet and discuss the programs they use. These groups generally include numerous computer users with valuable experience which you may be able to benefit from; someone in a user group may be able to answer a question in just a few minutes that would take you hours to figure out. User groups are lots of fun and don't cost much to attend. Often representatives from software companies come to demonstrate products and present information (sometimes they even give away software as a door prizes!). Groups can be located through computer periodicals, the phone book, calling the User Group Locator Line (see Appendix), or by asking at local computer stores.

Online Services

Online services, such as CompuServe, are also great sources of information. They do charge by the minute, but can save you valuable time. There are bulletin boards for all sorts of activities (including singles matchmaking), and many will give you a free hour or two to try out. You can also call and talk to a live person and find out more about the service. Ask at your user group for recommendations.

Employee Training

If you are still in a regular job, another way to increase your computer skills is to convince your present employer to pay for your training. Not only will you personally benefit from the extra education, but the more skills you have, the more valuable you will be as an employee.

STEP SIX: HOW DO YOU REPRESENT YOURSELF?

Business Cards, Stationery, and Promotional Literature

In order to be considered in business by your clients, you will need business cards, stationery, and promotional literature. These items promote and reflect who you are and who you are trying to reach, as well as providing a valuable sales tool.

A sales brochure is also a wonderful promotional tool to give potential customers when they call and ask you for information on your services. If they receive a brochure that details your expertise, background, and services, your business will easier to remember and relate to. If you cannot write a good brochure yourself, it is worth hiring someone to do it for you. The fee you pay your writer could easily be paid back with a few steady clients.

STEP SEVEN: WHAT HAVE YOU GOT TO SHOW THEM?

Clients like to see examples of what you do. For instance, if you create mailing lists for people, you can make up a mailing list of dummy names in order to display the types of labels and quality of print you provide.

You can make samples even if you are just starting out and have never sold your services before. For any kind of service you provide, you can make an outstanding portfolio of examples that will impress your clients. While you create the examples, you will learn how to use your programs better. Save your work for later use with Macros, templates, and style sheets.

STEP EIGHT: WHAT ARE YOUR PLANS?

You will need to set up a business plan, mainly for yourself, so that you know how much work you will need to bring in in order to make a profit. A plan is very useful to look at when you get confused and want to know what to do next.

A marketing strategy is also essential. You will need to get some idea of how to best reach the people you want to provide services to. Making a business plan and marketing strategy, along with records and information management, good business rules, and tricks and tips, are covered extensively in the following chapters.

CHAPTER 3 EXERCISES

1. Call your local city, county, and state offices to find out the necessary licenses for your business.
    a. Call your state board of equalization to find out if you need to charge sales tax.
    b. Check with a reliable source to find out about any laws you are unsure of.
    c. Apply and pay for the necessary licenses or variances.
2. Make a list of pros and cons of the locations you are thinking about and choose your location.
3. Make a list of twenty names for your company, and check with friends or coworkers to see what they think of them. A few days later ask them which names they remember.
    a. What company names have you never forgotten? Why?
4. What do you know about computer equipment and software? What do you need to know more about before you can make a decision?
5. Write up a 50-word description of your business.
6. Write a biography of your work history. List your skills and experience.
    a. What special skill do you have which would serve your clients?
7. Write up an outline for your brochure.
8. What kind of wonderful samples can you make to show your clients? Make up three projects and do them in the next two weeks.

☑ Checklist of First Steps

- ❏ Do you have a great location for your work and will it help you generate business?
- ❏ Have your researched your location in regard to local laws?
- ❏ Have you met the deadlines for making a listing in your yellow pages?
- ❏ Is your business name memorable, easy to understand? Would it fall at the beginning of an alphabetical list in a directory?
- ❏ Do you have business cards, stationery, and brochures that represent you in a professional and interesting manner?
- ❏ Do you have excellent samples of your work?
- ❏ Are you ready to set up business and marketing plans?

After you have read and done the exercises in Chapters 4 and 5:

- ❏ Have you bought or leased the best equipment and software to meet your needs?
- ❏ Do you know your software programs well enough to conduct your business?

4 ♦ SOFTWARE AWARENESS

THE DETERMINATOR

The type of business you have will determine the kind of computer software and equipment you will be using. For instance, suppose you want to start a word processing business. After you've researched what word processing software best suits your needs (and decided on what financial and database programs you will use to keep track of your records), you can determine the best system to run your software. That's why we call software, "The Determinator."

CHOOSING THE RIGHT SOFTWARE FOR YOU

Software is any program designed to perform specialized functions. There are thousands of software programs listed in *The Software Encyclopedia* and *The Macintosh Product Registry*. To find out about the most widely used applications, you can go to a specialty computer store, or read the numerous periodicals which rate and describe various software packages. Ask friends or coworkers which programs they find useful—and which they don't. Users groups, bulletin boards, and online services will also help you make a decision about what software is best for what you plan to do.

✏ **NOTE**: Beware of salespeople at software stores; they may not always understand exactly what you want and need. As a consultant I have had to fix many mistakes resulting from a misunderstanding of customers' needs on the part of the salesperson.

When buying software, you will need to know what you'll be using it for and also be aware of your needs, desires, and preferences. Some people just need the bare minimum in software, while

31

others want a refined system with lots of features that make it worth the high price. Software can cost anywhere from $20 to $700. If you will be using it often and if it works well, it can make your business more profitable—so you should make sure you have the package that is best suited to your needs.

Before you figure out what the best software is, you may have to shop around and do a little testing first. In this chapter, I will only cover the basic and most widely used types of software as a general guideline. Be sure to research the programs you want to use before you buy *anything*. I once ordered a software package without knowing its exact specification and found out once it arrived that I had to upgrade my computer to run it.

GENERAL QUESTIONS TO ASK WHEN CHOOSING SOFTWARE

- ➤ What kind of system does it run on the most efficiently?
- ➤ What version of DOS, Windows, or Mac operating system does it need to run?
- ➤ How much is it and how much do the upgrades generally cost?
- ➤ Does it do exactly what I want it to do?
- ➤ What features does it have?
- ➤ How much disk space does it take up?
- ➤ Is it compatible with other software I plan on using?
- ➤ Is it user friendly, or will I need more training?
- ➤ Does it have toll-free technical support? If so, for how many days does support last?
- ➤ Is it commonly used so that if I need to hire employees, I will not have to train them?
- ➤ Do I know other people who use it and who can help me if I need it?

- ➤ How much memory does it need to run the most efficiently?
- ➤ Can I try a demo?
- ➤ What print drivers does it come with, and what printers will it print to?
- ➤ Is it the most recent version of the software?

GENERAL TYPES OF SOFTWARE PACKAGES

Accounting/Financial—Income and expenses are input and accounting functions are performed automatically. Packages most often print checks, cash flow reports, and tax records.

Art Programs—Used for drawing and designs. They usually have tools to make circles, squares, lines, and special effects. Designs are drawn with a mouse or pointing device.

Database—Data is entered in a prescribed way and then can be used for other functions. For instance, you can put the name, age, and addresses of 1,000 people into a database program and then print labels for all the people who are between 25 and 30 who live in the state of Alabama. Common uses are for inventory, mailing lists, pricing, and research.

Desktop Publishing—Used to set type, place graphics, and design pages with information created in other programs. The computer screen acts as a giant pasteboard for all the elements.

Integrated Packages—Contain different types of multiple programs that work together (e.g. a word processing, spreadsheet, database, and communications program).

Operating System—The system used to run software on your computer.

Spreadsheet—Programs used to compare numbers and statistics. Mathematical formulas and data are input to create "what if" figures and mathematical functions.

Utilities—Supplemental programs which can make certain tasks easier or more efficient (e.g. file locators, hardware testing, grammar checkers, etc.).

Word processing—Programs in which you type in text, edit it, format it, and, if desired, merge it into other documents.

In the next pages, I will give you some information about each type of program, describe the individual programs, and list the manufacturers and phone numbers.

☞ REMINDER: Before you buy anything, research the program in a recent magazine or periodical. Computer software is always subject to change.

✐ NOTE: for IBM-compatible programs all programs are DOS programs unless they are marked (D/W), meaning they are DOS and Windows programs, or (W) for Windows.

ACCOUNTING/FINANCIAL PROGRAMS

You will need some form of accounting system in your business to reflect how you are doing financially and to help you prepare your taxes. There are two methods of accounting: cash and accrual. Cash is simpler and is sufficient for small businesses. Accrual requires more accounting time, but usually is more suitable for large businesses. If your business grows, you can switch to accrual. Ask your accountant for a recommendation.

In general, an accounting program can:

Automatically pay your monthly bills

Print up checks

Track income and expenses

Track receivables

Track inventory

Keep records of assets and liabilities

Measure business performance and health

📎 **NOTE**: I've divided the accounting programs into small business and bigger business sections. Only the small business listings include descriptions. When deciding on an accounting program for a bigger business, there are many, many variables you need to consider. I suggest that you consult an expert (your accountant or several reference sources) before choosing a program for a bigger business.

Accounting: Small Business Programs, IBM Compatible

Best Books (W), Teleware, (800) 322-6962—Easy to use.

Cash Biz (D/W), M-USA Business Systems, (800) 933-6872—For small service businesses that need to create checks and invoices but not payroll or inventory.

CA Simply Money, Computer Associates International, (800) 531-5236—Over two million free copies distributed.

DacEasy Light, DacEasy Inc., (800) 322-3279—A basic checkbook-like program with low system requirements.

Dac Instant Accounting (D/W), DacEasy Inc., (800) 322-3279—An easy, simple program.

Managing Your Money, MECA Software, (800) 820-7458—Full of features, including financial planning. Documentation. Tutorial is excellent—and fun.

Microsoft Money (W), Microsoft, (800) 426-9400 A simple program with a feature that allows you to modem to a compatible bank and communicate financially.

One-Write Plus, NEBS, (800) 388-8000—Based on the popular manual accounting method known as one-write (or the pegboard system).

Quicken, Intuit (D/W), (800) 624-8742—One of the most widely used and sold simple accounting packages. Very easy to learn but does not handle receivable in great detail. Excellent for keeping track of income and expenses for taxes. Often available on sale, it's good on value.

Make Money with Your PC!

Accounting: Bigger Business Programs, IBM Compatible

Accounting Works, NEBS, (800) 388-8000.

Accpac Simply Accounting, Computer Associates International, (800) 531-5236.

Access with Platinum (D/W), Platinum Desktop Software, (800) 999-1891.

Business Works, Manzanita Software Systems, (800) 447-5700.

DacEasy Bonus Pack, DacEasy Inc., (800) 322-3279.

Microsoft Profit (W), Microsoft, (800) 426-9400.

M.Y.O.B. (W), Teleware, (800) 322-6962.

Pacioli, M-USA Business Systems, (800) 933-6872.

Peachtree (D/W), Peachtree Software, (800) 247-3224.

Takin' Care of Business, Hooper International, (800) 542-4405.

Quick Books (D/W), Intuit, (800) 624-8742.

Accounting: Small Business Programs, Macintosh

Best Books, Teleware, (800) 322-6962—Easy to use, organized by task.

Check Writer Pro, Aatrix Software, (800) 426-0854—Will print on regular bank checks or any paper, and has extensive calculating features for figuring interest and fees.

Cash Ledger, Check Mark Software, (800) 225-0387—Good, stable, and dependable.

Hi! Finance, Aatrix Software, (800) 426-0854—Will print on regular bank checks or any paper, and has online tracking of stocks and mutual funds.

MacMoney, Survivor Software, (310) 410-9527—Has fast data entry and great reports.

Managing Your Money, MECA Software, (800) 820-7458—Full of features including financial planning. Documentation. Tutorial is fun and excellent.

Quicken, Intuit, (800) 624-8742—One of the most widely used and sold simple accounting packages. Very easy to learn but does not handle receivables in great detail. Excellent for keeping track of income and expenses for taxes.

Accounting: Bigger Business Programs, Macintosh

Accpac Simply Accounting, Computer Associates International, (800) 531-5236.

Dynamics, Great Plains Software, (800) 456-0025.

Multiledger, Check Mark Software, (800) 225-0387.

M.Y.O.B., Teleware, (800) 322-6962.

Peachtree for Macintosh, Peachtree Software, (800) 247-3224.

Satori Components, Satori Software, (206) 443-0765.

ART PROGRAMS: DESKTOP PUBLISHING & GRAPHICS

Desktop publishing programs are needed for professional designers and graphic artists. To do minor typesetting and low-end formatting, a word processing program should be sufficient.

Desktop Publishing Programs, IBM Compatible

Corel Ventura (W), Corel, (800) 772-6735—A real mean machine for technical and long documents. Rates high on indexing, outlining, making tables of contents, and adding graphics with captions. Includes a database publisher.

Frame Maker (W), Frame Technology, (800) U-4-FRAME—With its own word processor, it's great for demanding documents with a long life that need to be updated continually. Best known for long and technical documents.

PageMaker (W), Aldus, (800) 628-2320—Favored by many, rates high for text rotation, wrapping text around graphics, and "find and replace" functions. It is graphically oriented and best for shorter documents.

QuarkXPress (W), Quark Inc., (800) 788-7835—Many type adjustments. Tops for very sophisticated and color publishing.

Desktop Publishing Programs, Macintosh

Frame Maker, Frame Technology, (800) U-4-FRAME—With its own word processor, it's great for demanding documents with a long life which need to be updated continually. Best known for long and technical documents.

PageMaker, Aldus, (800) 628-2320—Simpler than Quark, has less adjustments, and is easier to learn.

QuarkXPress, Quark Inc.,(800) 788-7835—The powerhouse on the Mac. Has many adjustments. Tops for very sophisticated and color publishing.

Art & Drawing Programs, IBM Compatible

Arts & Letters (W), Computer Support Corp., (214) 661-8960—A lot of great clip art.

Canvas (W), Deneba Software, (800) 622-6827—Easy to use for nonartists and techie types.

Corel Draw! (W), Corel Systems Corp., (800) 772-6735—Highly rated. More than just an art program, can be used for photo editing, presentation graphics, charting, and animation.

Fractal Painter (W), Fractal Design, (408) 688-8800—Lets you paint with oil or watercolor, airbrush, use ink or pastels, or paint like Van Gogh on any kind of paper you like—all on your computer screen!

Micrographx Designer (W), Micrographx Inc., (800) 733-3729—Great for technical illustrators and artists.

Art & Drawing Programs, Macintosh

Adobe Illustrator, Adobe Systems Inc., (800) 833-6687—Has top text handing tools, drawing and charting capabilities. Widely used.

Aldus Freehand, Aldus Corp., (800) 628-2320—Similar to Adobe Illustrator. Great for graphic artists.

📳 Software Awareness

- **Canvas, Deneba Software, (800) 622-6827**—Inexpensive program with a lot of bells and whistles.
- **Fractal Painter, Fractal Design, (408) 688-8800**—Lets you paint with oil or watercolor, airbrush, use ink or pastels, or paint like Van Gogh on any kind of paper you like—all on your computer screen!
- **MacDraw Pro, Claris Corp., (800) 3-CLARIS**—Started out as an easy, simple program and now has added features, but still is not used as widely by professional artists as other programs.

DATABASES

Databases can save you thousands of hours of information management headaches. They help you keep track of all the things you need to remember—but can't—and sort everything out for you.

Flat File Databases, IBM Compatible

- **Alpha Four (D/W), Alpha Software, (800) 852-5950**—Has a good tutorial, is flexible, and handles complex tasks.
- **FileMaker Pro (W), Claris, (800) 3-CLARIS**—Very easy to use and even checks your spelling.
- **Q & A (D/W), Symantec Corp., (800) 441-7234**—Easy to learn and use. It comes with a word processor that makes mailing labels and mass mailings super simple.

Programmable Databases, IBM Compatible

- **Approach (W), Lotus Development, (800) 343-5414, (800) GO LOTUS (CANADA)**—A kinder and gentler relational database.
- **dBASE, Borland International, (800) 331-0877**—The first big database on the market, but requires knowledge of its language in order to program.
- **FoxPro (D/W), Microsoft, (800) 426-9400**—Fast and powerful. It has a user-friendly interface.
- **Paradox (D/W), Borland International (800) 331-0877**—Has a lot of power and the ability to query by example.

Superbase (W), Software Publishing Corp., (800) 234-2500—Multi-user and graphic capabilities.

Flat File Databases, Macintosh

FileMaker Pro, Claris Corp., (800) 3-CLARIS—Very popular and easy to use.

Panorama, Pro Vue, (800) 966-7878—Flexible, powerful, and has amazing clairvoyance feature.

Programmable Database, Macintosh

4th Dimension, ACI US, (408) 252-4444—Easy to use on a basic level. Can be programmed to do amazing things by a programmer.

FoxPro, Microsoft, (800) 426-9400—Well rated and highly regarded.

INTEGRATED SOFTWARE

When you're starting out, it's nice to have easy programs that all work together. Integrated packages are a great start, but can be frustrating when you outgrow them. On the other hand, if your needs are not that great, an integrated package may be all you need.

Integrated Software, IBM Compatible

Microsoft Works (D/W), Microsoft, (800) 426-9400—Simple, easy-to-use word processing, spreadsheet, database, and communications software.

Integrated Software, Macintosh

Claris Works, Claris (800) 3-CLARIS—An everything-but-the-kitchen-sink array of good tools: spreadsheet, database, word processing, presentation graphics, and paint program—all rolled up into one easy and practical program.

Great Works, Symantec, (800) 441-7234—Has a word processing module that can do outlining, as well as a point module.

SOFTWARE AWARENESS

Microsoft Works (D/W), Microsoft, (800) 426-9400—Simple, easy-to-use word processing, spreadsheet, database, and communications software.

OPERATING SYSTEMS

An operating system is the basic program which controls a computer's operation. You will need an operating system to run all of your software.

Operating Systems, IBM Compatible

DOS, Microsoft, (800) 426-9400—Most widely used, and should come with your system.

OS/2, IBM Corporation, (800) 426-3333—Favored by corporate users, it will run both DOS and Windows applications.

Windows, Microsoft, (800) 426-9400—Turns your IBM or clone into something like a Mac with a graphical user interface (GUI). With it, you can run different programs simultaneously. Needed to run Excel, PageMaker, and Corel Draw!

Operating Systems, Macintosh

System 7.x, Apple, (800) 776-2333—Lots of great features. Very state-of-the-art.

Soft PC, Insignia Solutions, (800) 848-7677—Enables a Macintosh to run IBM-compatible programs.

SPREADSHEET PROGRAMS

For number crunching and charting, these programs are valuable business tools.

Spreadsheets, IBM Compatible

Lotus 123 (D/W), Lotus Development (800) 343-5414, (800) GO LOTUS (in Canada)—Several different versions exist. A good everyday spreadsheet, it is widely used, but is not exactly user-friendly. The Windows version has some neat features and is easier to use.

Lotus Improv (W), Lotus Development, (800) 343-5414, (800) GO LOTUS (in Canada)—A multidimensional spreadsheet program that is easy to use.

Microsoft Excel (W), Microsoft, (800) 426-9400—Runs in Windows and has sophisticated analytical features with ease of use which is why *PC Magazine* gave it "Editors' Choice."

Quattro Pro (D/W), Borland International, (800) 331-0877—Can use multiple files, make graphs, and use dBASE and Paradox data.

Spreadsheets, Macintosh

Lotus 123, Lotus Development (800) 343-5414—Impressive functions, but a little slower than Excel at calculation.

Macula, Bravo, (510) 841-8552—Basic spreadsheet program with no charting capabilities.

Microsoft Excel, Microsoft, (800) 426-9400—The best. Widely used.

Resolve, Claris, (800) 3-CLARIS—Has great 3-D charts.

UTILITY PROGRAMS

Since programs are specialized, no one program can do everything for you, which is why you may want to invest in a utility program to supplement your general system.

Utility Programs, IBM Compatible

CheckIt PRO (D/W), TouchStone, (800) 531-0450—Top utility for diagnosing technical problems and conflicts, especially if you are installing hardware.

Faxworks Pro (D/W), Soften Inc., (404) 984-8088—Handy fax program that compresses incoming faxes and can also turn them into text.

HiJack Pro (W), Inset, (800) 374-6738—Useful conversion utility for people who use many different graphic programs.

SOFTWARE AWARENESS

Norton Anti-Virus, Symantec (800)441-7234—Catches those nasty bugs before they infect your system.

Norton Desktop for Windows (W), Symantec, (800) 441-7234—A more user-friendly shell for Windows that has backup and antivirus capabilities.

Norton Utilities, Symantec, (800) 441-7234—Has lots of tools that make computing easier and less stressful.

Qemm386, Quarterdeck, (800) 354-3222—If you are using Windows, it will help you configure RAM and make your programs run faster.

Stacker (D/W), Stac, (800) 522-7822—Compresses your data, almost tripling your disk space, which you can fill up all over again.

Uninstaller, Micro Help Inc., (800) 922-3383—A must for Windows users who don't like spending hours uninstalling Windows Programs.

Winfax Pro (W), Delrina, (800) 268-6082—Helps you manage incoming and outgoing faxes.

Utility Programs, Macintosh

MacTools, Central Point Software, (800) 445-4208—Easy to use and fast! Provides data recovery, trash recovery, virus protection, and backup.

Norton Utilities, Symantec, (800) 441-7234—Highly recommended by *MacUser*, it optimizes your hard disk and helps protect and restore data.

QuickKeys, CE Software, (800) 523-7638—A powerful work horse that makes creating shortcuts and macros a simple process.

SAM (Symantec Anti-Virus for Macintosh), Symantec, (800) 441-7234—Powerful and effective antivirus program.

StuffIt Deluxe, Aladin Systems, (408) 761-6200—The most popular Mac data compression utility.

WORD PROCESSING PROGRAMS

The days of using a typewriter are over, even for envelopes. Word processing programs perform all sorts functions, including checking your spelling and helping you correct your mistakes.

Word Processing, IBM Compatible

Ami Pro (W), Lotus Development, (800) 831-9679—Winner of numerous awards. Popular for graphics.

Microsoft Word, Microsoft, (800) 426-9400—Has powerful formatting and style features.

Microsoft Word for Windows (W), Microsoft, (800) 426-9400—Has a lot of high-end features including styles, formatting, and automatic typo correction. Good if you are also using Excel and other Microsoft products.

WordPerfect for DOS, WordPerfect Corp., (800) 451-5151—Despite the increasing popularity of Windows programs, still the king of word processors. Supported with excellent technical assistance by very nice operators.

WordPerfect for Windows, WordPerfect Corp., (800) 451-5151—Powerful file management and compatibility with DOS WordPerfect.

WordStar(D/W), WordStar International, (800) 227-5609—Was the first widely-used program, but has since lost its market share. Uses keyboard codes which, once learned, are wonderful. Tried and true WordStar users will not use anything else.

Word processing, Macintosh

MacWrite, Claris Corp., (800) 3-CLARIS—Good basic program.

Microsoft Word, Microsoft, (800) 426-9400—Widely used and has many high-end features.

WordPerfect, WordPerfect Corp., (800) 451-5151—Great for IBM converts and has super toll-free technical support.

SOFTWARE AWARENESS

Nisus, Nisus Software, (800) 922-2993—Great features, great technical support, and automatically saves and makes backups.

WriteNow, WordStar International, (800) 227-5609—Fast, reliable, and simple.

HOW SUITE IT IS!

As software wars continue, the latest arsenal in competition software selling is the "suite" in which you get several compatible software programs for an unbelievably low price. Sometimes a suite will be everything you need and then some. However, most of the programs in the suite may be exactly what you want, while others may just sit on your shelf or hard disk. See what suites contain the software you want and then decide if it buying one is a good deal.

Suites, IBM Compatible

Borland Office (W), Burland International, (800) 331-0877—Includes Burland products and WordPerfect—all in one.

Lotus Suite (W), Lotus Development, (800) 831-9679—Comes with a highly rated calendar program, Lotus Organizer.

Microsoft Office (W), Microsoft, (800) 426-9400—A bundle of Microsoft products which all work well together.

Suites, Macintosh

Microsoft Office, Microsoft, (800) 426-9400—A bundle of Microsoft products which all work well together.

SHAREWARE

Low cost shareware is available for a variety of different functions. However, you will have limited support, training availability, and compatibility. For programs that you do not use frequently, shareware is sufficient. Since it is inexpensive, you can always try it just for fun. There are excellent shareware utilities which perform all sorts of neat functions—just remember to ask questions.

✏ **NOTE:** Shareware is not free. The authors allow the software to circulate so people can try it out. If you like it, you are expected to pay a registration fee which enables you to obtain upgrades, technical support, and other information.

WARNING..

Although it may seem this chapter has mentioned every imaginable software package available, only the most popular and best reviewed products have been included. If you can't find what you are looking for in this book, check other reference sources for more information.

•••••••••••••••••••••••

Learning about your first software programs may seem difficult at first, but if you keep asking questions you'll learn quickly. Take your time with the exercises so you can achieve "total software awareness."

📖 CHAPTER 4 EXERCISES

1. Check off the software that looks the best to you.
2. Call the software companies and ask for information on the programs you checked.
3. Look up your chosen software in computer periodicals, and read about its features. See how it is rated. Do you still think it is the best choice?
4. Look in computer publications or your local newspaper to see if there is a user group for the software you've selected. If so, go to a meeting.
5. Go to a computer store and see if you can be given a demonstration on the software you've chosen.
6. Ask your friends who use the software what they think about it.
7. After you have chosen your software, find out what system is needed to use it most efficiently. Be sure to write down all the hardware requirements to use when you buy your hardware.

MAKE MONEY WITH YOUR PC!

💾 *Software Reminders*

☞ Make sure your computer insurance policy covers software.

☞ **ALWAYS** ask if what you are buying is compatible with your system and other software.

☞ Before you buy, ask if the software is the latest version, and when the next version is coming out. (Sometimes you can miss an upgrade by a few days.)

☞ Register your software immediately.

☞ Install your software as soon as you buy it. If you install it months later and it is faulty, you may not be able to return it.

☞ **ALWAYS** backup your software programs. Make sure copies and originals are kept in a safe place.

☞ Beware of bootlegged programs. Check for viruses, especially if you don't know where the programs have been.

☞ Back up! Back UP! BACK UP!

5 ✦ HARDWARE MADE EASY

Meet Your New Best Friend, Your Computer

When you choose your friends, you want them to be reliable, easy to be with, trustworthy, and compatible. The same is true for your computer. You will be dependent on this machine for your living. Therefore, you only want the best, and you want it compatible with what you are doing. If you want the latest software programs to run at their optimal speed it is best to buy state-of-the-art equipment. If you already own a computer, you may discover that your computer needs to be upgraded to run the software you want to use. If this is the case, be sure to shop around before you make any changes; sometimes upgrading your old equipment can cost you more than buying an entirely new system.

Buying computers and software can turn out to be a major undertaking—which is great for computer consultants like myself because people find it easier and more efficient to pay someone who is an expert to do all the work. However, if you do not have the money to hire a consultant, you will have to choose hardware and software by yourself. You may be living with your computer ten years or more, so ask as many questions as possible before you buy.

The first lesson I learned when buying a computer was not to listen to someone who is not an expert. When I bought my first computer, I planned on using it for word processing. My computer consultant advised me to get an XT because I wouldn't need anything better. Within six months, I was frustrated because I had outgrown my computer's capacity. Since the system had cost

$1,000, I was not able to afford to replace it for quite some time and wish to this day that I had bought a faster system.

In the following pages, I describe each part of the system you will need, followed by questions to ask yourself and your dealer. You can read these sections at your own speed. You can also take them with you when you go to computer stores. It may seem like too much information at first, but pretty soon you will be talking technobabble with the rest of us. Remember, what you want to do with the system determines what you buy; often installing new products or upgrading not only costs more but takes your precious computer away so you can't work and make money with it. It is usually less expensive to buy all your equipment at once with pre-installed software.

MAC VS. IBM COMPATIBLES

There has been much written about which platform is better and the truth is, it is a matter of style and operation. The best way to choose a platform is to check out both and do a test drive to see what you are most comfortable with. Macs are heavily dependent on mice and hand/eye coordination and are very user-friendly. IBM compatibles are not as user-friendly, but can be made more graphically oriented by running Windows.

[?] QUESTIONS TO ASK WHEN CONSIDERING A MAC VS. IBM COMPATIBLE COMPUTER

➤ Am I not very technically minded? (If so, go for the Mac's simplicity and usability.)

➤ Do I already know one system and have programs for that system?

➤ Does the software I want to use run better on either system?

CPUS

The CPU or central processing unit is a chip connected to the electronic circuitry (the system or motherboard) which processes the information you are entering, creating, and/or retrieving.

(Depending on who you are talking to, the CPU may also mean the entire computer box, excluding the keyboard and monitor.) In either a Mac or an IBM clone, the faster the CPU model, the faster the computer works. Often the speed is measured in Megahertz (MHz), millions of cycles per second.

The use of electricity is also important for CPUs. The typical computer uses about $35 worth of electricity a year for a system that is on eight hours a day, compared to $105 per year for a system that is never turned off. The EPA created the "Energy Star" program for systems that conserve energy. These systems should be considered if, in the long run, you want to save energy and money.

[?] Questions to Ask When You Buy a CPU

- ➤ How fast is it?
- ➤ How much memory can I add?
- ➤ What kind of warranty/guarantee does it come with?
- ➤ Will I be able to upgrade when something new comes out?
- ➤ Does it come with DOS or an operating system?
- ➤ How many slots and ports does it have?
- ➤ What type of service does the dealer offer? Is it worth it?
- ➤ Is it the best speed for the kinds of operations I want to do in two years?
- ➤ Is it energy efficient?

HARD DISKS

Hard disks or hard drives store your data and software programs. As programs get more complicated, they take up more room. I've heard stories of people who, no matter how large a hard disk they have, always keep it full. Therefore, it is a good idea to get a lot of hard disk space—more than you think you'll use and then some. You'll also want a drive with a fast access time (the number of milliseconds it takes to locate and retrieve stored information).

✏ **NOTE:** A bit of information about bits and bytes:

> *A bit is the smallest possible unit of information.*
>
> *A byte is 8 bits.*
>
> *A Kilobyte is about 1,024 bytes*
>
> *A Megabyte is 1,048,576 bytes.*
>
> *A gigabyte is a billion bytes.*

[?] QUESTIONS TO ASK WHEN BUYING A HARD DISK

➤ What is the megabyte capacity?

➤ How much does it cost per megabyte?

➤ What is the access time?

➤ Does it come with mounting brackets and cables?

➤ Is it compatible with what I already have?

➤ Will the dealer install it for free?

MEMORY

RAM or Random Access Memory is the amount of information that can be held in the computer's memory buffer at any given time. If you will be doing a lot of graphics or intensive number operations, the more RAM the better. In either Macs or IBM clones, you should have at least four megabytes of RAM, but depending on your applications, you may need much more.

When you buy an entire system the memory is usually installed for free. If you bring it back later for more, they will probably charge you for the installation and the additional memory.

[?] QUESTIONS TO ASK WHEN BUYING MEMORY

➤ How much space is available for more memory later?

➤ Does my system use clone memory chips or need specialized name-brand chips?

FLOPPY DISK DRIVES

On the IBM compatibles you will have your choice of 5¼-inch and 3½-inch disk drives. It is best to get both because you may be getting both kinds of disks from your clients. (The price for an extra drive is worth it.)

If you buy a used IBM compatible computer, make sure that the 5¼ drive has a 1.2 megabyte capacity and the 3½ has a 1.44 megabyte capacity. In both Macs and IBM compatibles, the higher capacity drives will read information off the lower drives, but the lower drives can't read the higher drives.

Most Macs come with an internal 3½-inch disk drive and use 3½-inch disks exclusively.

MONITORS

Once upon a time, there were just monochrome monitors which came in one size. Not any more. Now, not only are there color and monochrome monitors available, but they come in all different sizes and resolutions. The most common monitors for IBM compatibles are VGAs (Video Graphics Adapters) and SVGAs (Super Video Graphics Adapters), which have a much higher resolution than VGAs. Multifrequency monitors can usually display both VGA and SVGA, or more than one resolution or frequency.

Monochrome monitors are sufficient for word processing, but if you're planning on using graphic programs, you may want to consider a color monitor. You'll also want to consider what monitor size will be best for the work that you do. Obviously a larger monitor will allow you to see more of your work on the screen at once. You may also want to consider these features, which make staring at a monitor less stressful on your eyes: a high resolution (the number of dots of light, pixels, a monitor can display); a small dot pitch (the space between the pixels—the smaller the space the sharper the image); a fast refresh rate (how fast the image is redrawn on the screen); a non-interlaced monitor (interlaced monitors spray every other line, creating a vibrating image or flicker); a flat screen, which reduces glare and distortion.

Shopping and looking at monitors for either platform will help you decide what the best type is for you. Notice the differences between the different monitors in the store. Then ask the salesperson about them.

⸮ QUESTIONS TO ASK WHEN YOU BUY A MONITOR

- Is it compatible with my system and my software?
- What is the resolution?
- What size is it?
- How many shades of gray does it show?
- How many colors does it display?
- What is the refresh rate?
- Is it interlaced or non-interlaced?
- If my computer is an IBM Compatible, is the monitor VGA? SVGA? Is it a multifrequency monitor?
- Does it have antiglare glass? Is the screen flat or curved?
- Can the monitor be adjusted and tilted any way I like it?
- Can my system have more than one monitor?
- What's the warranty like?
- Does it meet the latest standards for ELF (extremely low frequency) and VLF (very low frequency) radiation?
- Is it energy efficient?
- Does is connect to one of my ports, or do I need an adapter?

VIDEO CARDS OR BOARDS

To run the monitor you will need a compatible video processor card. Your monitor will run faster if there is one megabyte or more of memory on the video card.

🖫 Hardware Made Easy

✐ NOTE: Macs come with a video chip on the system board which will run most monitors. Certain monitors, however, require a special video card.

❓ Questions to Ask When You Buy a Video Adapter Card

➤ Is it compatible with the rest of my equipment?

➤ How much memory does it have?

➤ Will it accelerate graphics?

➤ How fast does it work?

➤ What kinds of reviews did the product receive?

➤ If I have an IBM compatible, does it have VGA, SVGA, and non-interlaced capabilities? Is it local bus? (Local bus video cards connect directly into the CPU's processor, making it work faster.)

KEYBOARDS

There are numerous manufacturers of keyboards. Some have the function keys on the top, some have them on the side, and some have trackballs on them. If you have never used a keyboard, be sure to try out the one you are planning to buy before you buy it.

If you are an experienced keyboarder, you might want to consider an ergonomically designed keyboard. This book could not have been written without an ergonomic keyboard from the Kinesis Corporation. I have set up the keyboard to reduce the stress on my arms by using a foot peddle for some functions. It has made writing long documents (like books) much easier.

MICE & TRACKBALLS

Mice and trackballs are pointing devices you use to move the cursor around on the screen. They are like keyboards in that they have different touches and feels to them, so you need to choose one that feels right to you. Try both out before you buy.

[?] QUESTIONS TO ASK WHEN YOU BUY MICE & TRACKBALLS

➤ Which do I prefer, the feel of the mouse or the trackball?

➤ Is it compatible with all the software I am using?

➤ Do I want it to be cordless?

➤ Is it made by a company that has been in business for a while and will be available for service.

LASER PRINTERS

Because of their incredibly clear output, laser printers have become one of the most popular printers available. When buying a laser printer, it is important to consider the resolution, or dots per inch (dpi). The higher the dpi, the sharper the image. Therefore, if you will be doing detail-oriented output, you will want to consider a printer with a high dpi.

There are laser printers available for a fairly low price. However, before you consider buying a low-end brand, realize that you may be using the printer for several years and you will need to buy toner cartridges for that printer. If the printer is not very popular and the manufacturer stops making that printer, you will have difficulty buying cartridges. I met a consultant who bought an odd brand laser printer several years ago that never became popular. Few software programs had drivers for the printer. She couldn't upgrade it to have it use various fonts and had to buy a Hewlett Packard to complete a project she was working on. A bargain printer should at least be compatible with a major brand or your software will not run it.

Some printers come with resident fonts. PostScript printers usually come with two or more megabytes of memory and have 35 scaleable resident fonts. Thirty-five fonts may seem like a lot, but considering most type faces have a bold, bold italic, and italic, each considered a font, that leaves about nine families of type. In November of every year, *PC Magazine* produces an excellent issue devoted entirely to reviewing printers. If you can get a copy from the library, it will help you choose the right printer for your needs.

✏ **LASER PRINTER USERS PLEASE NOTE**: There is a heating unit in some models of laser printers similar to a toaster oven that is kept hot all the time so you can print faster. If you do not have a low-watt wait state mode on your laser, turn it off when you are not using it and save on your electric bill.

❓ QUESTIONS TO ASK WHEN YOU BUY A LASER PRINTER

➤ Is it compatible with my system and software?

➤ What is the resolution? How many dots per inch?

➤ What kind of port on my computer does it connect to?

➤ How much memory does it have?

➤ How much space does it take up?

➤ How many pages per minute does it print?

➤ What is the maximum number of pages it can print per month?

➤ What is the cost per page?

➤ What size paper does can it print on?

➤ Does it print envelopes? Labels? Transparencies?

➤ Can it print on both sides of the paper?

➤ What does a printout of the resident fonts look like?

➤ Does it have a power-saving mode?

INK JET PRINTERS

Ink jet printers spray ink onto a page through tiny nozzles in the print head. They can cost half the price of a laser printer, but the per page cost can be almost double. The quality of the output looks very good at first but a close examination with a magnifying glass will show smudges, waviness in the text, ink bleeding, and extra ink spray (a.k.a. satellites). They do, however, do a nice economical job of color printing. Before you buy one of these mid-level printers, look at the quality of the output and see if it meets your standards.

✏ **NOTE**: I have been told by ink jet users that if you use quality ink jet paper, there are no satellites and the quality of the print improves.

❓ QUESTIONS TO ASK WHEN YOU BUY AN INK JET PRINTER

- ➤ How many dots per inch does it print?
- ➤ What is the per page cost?
- ➤ How many pages per minute does it print?
- ➤ Is it compatible with all my software?
- ➤ Can it print on envelopes, labels, transparencies, and different size papers?
- ➤ Does it have resident fonts? If so, how many and what are they?
- ➤ How does the output look?

DOT MATRIX PRINTERS

Dot matrix printers were once the only affordable printers for home use. Even though they make a lot of noise, they are excellent for running long spreadsheets and tractor-fed labels, and can be good for printing multiple documents, NCR forms, and wide items. Some printers can also give very nice near-letter-quality text, which is fine for proofing. But unfortunately, nowadays, many people are spoiled and expect laser output. So, if you are doing anything like desktop publishing, you will need a laser printer.

❓ QUESTIONS TO ASK WHEN YOU BUY A DOT MATRIX PRINTER

- ➤ How clear is the output?
- ➤ What size paper can it print on?
- ➤ Does it come with a sheet feeder?
- ➤ How many characters per second does it print?
- ➤ How loud is it? Can you muffle the noise?
- ➤ Are ribbons easily replaceable?

- What fonts does it come with?
- What is the per page cost?
- Is it compatible with my software and system?

SCANNERS

Scanners work something like a camera; they convert an image into a computer file. They are excellent for line art (photographs and color pictures require more sophistication to get great output), and are necessary to run Optical Character Recognition programs which turn documents into easy-to-use computer files. They are something you might want to invest in if you will be entering extensive information from preprinted documents; or if you are a desktop publisher or graphic designer.

There are several different types of scanners: Hand held for line art (low dpi); hand held gray scaling; bed scanners; gray scale bed scanners; and color bed scanners.

Questions to Ask When Buying a Scanner

- Is it compatible with my system and software?
- Will I have to buy photo editing or conversion software to use it?
- Is there toll-free assistance available?

MODEMS

With a modem, all you have to do is connect it to a phone line and you will be able to log on to bulletin boards and online services. For instance, my library has an online catalog which has saved me many unnecessary trips by enabling me to find out if the book I wanted was on loan or not. Since the online catalog is available 24 hours a day, I have also used it late at night to check on book titles and authors.

With a modem I can download files from bulletin boards or from coworkers. I can also submit articles in a ready-to-use format to magazines via my phone and not have to worry about the post office getting my article there on time.

Modems can be either external or internal and are very inexpensive. If you will be using the modem often, it is best to buy the fastest speed available to save telephone bills and time.

[?] QUESTIONS TO ASK WHEN YOU BUY A MODEM

- Will it fit on my system board?
- Is it compatible with the industry standard?
- Does it come with software?
- How fast is it?
- Does it have a guarantee?
- Can I adjust the volume from the outside or do I need special software to do so?
- Is it external or internal? Which is easier for me to set up?

FAX MODEMS

For about $50 extra, many modems come with a fax card. A fax modem, which can cost less than $100, can save you time and money. For instance, I frequently fax bids, memos, and pertinent information to clients. On top of everything else, a fax modem actually faxes clearer images than a regular fax machine because it doesn't have to be translated by a fax machine reader. You can also print the faxes you receive on plain paper, without that ugly photo fax paper curl. All in all it's a good deal.

[?] QUESTIONS TO ASK WHEN YOU BUY A FAX MODEM

- Is it compatible with my system and software?
- Is it internal or external?
- Can it send and receive?
- Does it come with software?
- Can it be programmed to send and receive faxes when I'm not around?
- Can I fax graphics from my graphics programs?

TAPE BACKUP DRIVES

There are many horror stories out there about companies and individuals who have lost months and even years of work because they did not backup up their work. Hard disks can crash. The average life expectancy of a hard disk is around five years, while some have been known to commit "hari kiri" in less than six months—taking their life and all your work with them.

Your computer can also be stolen. An extremely high percentage of computer insurance claims are due to theft. I know of a graphic artist and a composer who both had their computers stolen: The graphic artist had her files on a backup tape and lost no work; the composer did not have a backup and lost eight years' worth of songs and charts.

While you can make backups of your work on floppy disks, doing so can take a long time. Tape backup drives are fast and can be programmed to automatically make backups of your work at the same time every day. The cost of these drives is relatively inexpensive and well worth the investment.

[?] QUESTIONS TO ASK WHEN YOU BUY A TAPE BACKUP DRIVE

➤ Is it compatible with my system and software?

➤ What kind of port does it connect to?

➤ Is it an internal or external drive?

➤ Is it portable?

➤ Does it need a special adapter card?

➤ How fast does it back up information?

➤ How many megabytes of data will one cartridge hold?

➤ Does it come with software?

➤ Does it come with cables or mounting hardware?

➤ Where can I buy the cassettes?

MULTIMEDIA

A multimedia system combines sounds and images to perform a variety of functions. For instance, there are new programs coming out that make your spreadsheet say the numbers out loud so that you can check your figures against a hard copy. There are also programs that take your voice commands, or turn your voice into characters. Multimedia is a new field and we can't be sure what new and exciting applications there will be in the future.

The basic components of a multimedia system: a CD-ROM drive, a sound card, speakers or headphones, and a microphone. Many computer dealers put together entire multimedia systems for you, in which all the components are compatible. This is usually the easiest and most economical way of purchasing a multimedia system. There are also multimedia kits in which all the components to upgrade your system come together.

[?] QUESTIONS TO ASK WHEN YOU BUY A MULTIMEDIA SYSTEM OR MULTIMEDIA UPGRADE KIT

➤ Does it meet the most current standards?

➤ Is it compatible with the software I want to use?

➤ Does it come with software?

➤ How has the system been reviewed in industry publications?

CD-ROM DRIVES

CD-ROMs (Compact Disk—Read Only Memory) can hold up to 680 megabytes of data and are being used widely for many applications such as databases, long technical documentation, animation clip art, photos, fonts, and reference material. However, these applications require *beaucoup* disk space. There are internal and external CD-ROM drives, and the faster the drive the better. The speed of your CD-ROM is measured by how quickly it can access information (its access rate).

[?] QUESTIONS TO ASK WHEN YOU BUY A CD-ROM DRIVE

- ➤ Is it compatible with my system and software?
- ➤ What is the access rate?
- ➤ Does it meet the latest standards for multimedia?
- ➤ Is it compatible with the CDs I want to use?
- ➤ Does it have an automatic lens cleaning mechanism or a dust protection door?
- ➤ Does it have standard audio output jacks, volume control, and audio software?
- ➤ Is it portable?

SOUND CARDS

Sound cards enable your computer to record and make sounds that can be connected to text and graphics. The cards are connected into either an 8- or 16-bit slot on the motherboard of your computer. (Macs come with sound capabilities already installed.)

[?] QUESTIONS TO ASK WHEN YOU BUY A SOUND CARD

- ➤ Is it 8- or 16-bit? (16-bit cards usually have a better sound.)
- ➤ Does it come with a good microphone? What does it sound like?
- ➤ Does it come with earphones or headphones? How do they sound?
- ➤ Does it filter out the power from my computer?
- ➤ Does it produce all frequencies, including the high and low frequencies?
- ➤ For music, does it use wave table lookup (digitized recordings of actual instruments)?
- ➤ Does the board ground easily?

SPEAKERS

Speakers can make a big difference in the quality of sound on your system. If you're lucky and have a stereo near, you could patch your sound into your stereo. If not, you'll need magnetically shielded speakers. Most speakers that are made specifically for computers are magnetically shielded.(Macs already come with speakers installed, although some audiophiles like to supplement them with external speakers.)

? QUESTIONS TO ASK WHEN YOU BUY SPEAKERS

➤ Are they shielded?

➤ How do they sound?

➤ Is the output clear and free of distortion?

➤ Do they fit on my desk?

➤ Are the controls easy to use and reachable?

➤ How many watts per channel do they have?

OH WHERE OH WHERE DO I BUY MY SYSTEM?

There are many places you can buy a computer system: local dealers, superstores, office warehouses, electronics stores, and computer swap meets or shows. Each place has advantages and disadvantages. I once bought a system from a dealer who was located over an hour away from me. The prices were excellent, but when I had problems with the system, I had to drive over there several times. Since then, I have relied on a dealer who was recommended to me by another consultant, located only a few minutes from my office.

Professional and personal referrals are always a good source in finding a reliable place to purchase your computer. For instance, there are usually members of users groups who have their own computer gurus to recommend. Magazines also often review various name-brand computers, direct-mail systems, and components. If you live in a small town or outside of the U.S., direct mail may be a good choice for you, but remember you will have to pay shipping. If you want to purchase your system from a superstore, make sure you know exactly what you want and why. Wherever you buy your system, there will be questions to ask and the first one is "What is your return policy?"

[?] QUESTIONS TO ASK YOUR COMPUTER SYSTEMS DEALERSHIP

- ➤ What is your return policy?
- ➤ Does your equipment have a warranty? For how long?
- ➤ Do you install hardware and software for free?
- ➤ Do you offer discounts on software packages when I buy a system?
- ➤ How many years have you been in business?
- ➤ Do you have references in my field?
- ➤ Can I upgrade your systems with standard clone components or only with your brand?
- ➤ Do you offer toll-free technical support?
- ➤ Do you have in-house repair facilities?
- ➤ Do you test your systems before shipping?
- ➤ Can you answer all of my questions?

MAKE YOUR DECISIONS UNREGRETTABLE

After buying a personal computer, many people wish that they had bought better systems. In a buyer remorse study by Channel Marketing in Carollton Texas of 1,000 IBM and compatible users, many buyers wished they had purchased more expansion slots, a better quality monitor (with a higher dpi), more Random Access Memory (RAM), a larger hard drive, and two floppy disk drives. Many users who later tried to upgrade their systems found either that it wasn't possible or that the cost of upgrading the system was almost the same as buying a new one. Channel Marketing (and yours truly) advises buyers to consider not only what they want to do now with the computer, but what they'll want to do for the next couple of years.

OTHER PROBLEMS TO THINK ABOUT

Make sure that you do not plug your computer directly into an outlet. If there is a power surge, it may blow out one of your boards. Buy a surge protector when you buy the system. There are also power units that enable you to turn separate parts of your system on and off.

PROTECT YOUR EQUIPMENT

A client of mine bought a sparkling new HP laser printer and did not invest $10 to buy a cover. It is in a factory and dust blows into the printer. When I opened it up, after a few months, it was coated with dust. Dust is an excellent conductor and since the circuitry can be harmed by electromagnetic energy, that dust may eventually affect the workings of the printer. If you are in a dusty environment be sure to cover up your equipment. (Keyboards can also be affected by the dust, and covers for them are very inexpensive.)

INSURE YOUR COMPUTER

If your business is totally reliant on your computer and it is stolen, or damaged in an earthquake or fire, you may lose your entire business. Therefore invest the small sum it costs to insure your computer.

WARNING..

One more caveat about buying computer equipment: Be sure to check all the preceding information with an updated source before you buy *anything*. Computer technology is advancing so rapidly that within six months, a feature that was so expensive no one wanted to buy it can become affordable and mainstream. Magazines, such as *PC Computing*, *PC Magazine*, *PC World*, *MacUser*, *Macworld*, and *Info World*, are available at your library and are excellent reference sources.

✍ CHAPTER 5 EXERCISES

1. Go to several computer stores, office warehouses, or electronic stores, or call a direct seller, and look at systems (in person or via catalog).
2. Decide on the system you want.
3. Call several vendors to find the best price. Tell the dealers you call the other prices you have been offered. More than likely, they will beat the offer. (NOTE: If you are not going to use your system immediately, wait on asking for prices. The cost of hardware is constantly dropping.)
4. Make a list of all of the equipment you need and write the cost of each item next to it. Total it up and decide how much money you need to invest.
5. If you do not have the money now, is there a way you can save a certain amount each month and have it in a year? Can you establish credit now, while you are at your present job? If you are eligible and can get a loan, will you be able to cover the extra expense?

🖳 Hardware Reminders

☞ Be sure to keep your manuals and receipts for all parts of your system in a safe place.

☞ Save all your boxes and foam packaging just in case you need to send it back to the dealer.

☞ Theft proof your system by engraving or scratching your driver's license number on it somewhere for easy identification.

☞ Insure your computer as soon as you get it.

☞ If you have doubts about your dealer, check with the Better Business Bureau to see if there have been complaints against them.

☞ After you set up your computer station, make sure that the cables are out of the way so no one can trip over them.

6 ♦ PAIN IN THE NECK AVOIDANCE

ONLY YOU CAN PREVENT COMPUTER-RELATED PAIN

As I write this, my wrists are wrapped in black wrist braces, I wear special computer glasses, and a telephone headset is planted in my hair by my ears. My arms rest on swivel arm supports that come out of my ergonomic workstation; I have two different footrests; I'm wearing a shoulder harness; I have two back support pillows that I change often; and I sit on a special pillow I made for my condition that I refer to as "computer butt." (The pain starts you-know-where and goes right up into my neck, shoulders, and arms.)

Why all this paraphernalia? Why do I look like an extraterrestrial android? I suffer from something many computer users get called CTDs (Cumulative Trauma Disorders) and RSIs (Repetitive Strain Injuries). All the years I hacked away happily without even adjusting my chair have taken their toll on me. There used to be days I was doubled over in pain and could not move. Fortunately, after years of trying every ergonomic device I could find, doing yoga every day, and seeing a chiropractor regularly, I am almost able to work in comfort.

The figures regarding computer-related pain are phenomenal. In a study at *Newsday*, 40% of keyboard users reported symptoms of CTDs. The National Institute for Occupational Safety and Health estimates that half of all office workers in the United States are at risk for RSI. As many as 46% of secretaries and 36% of word processors experience symptoms of carpal tunnel syndrome. There is, however, good news. If you practice ergonomic computing, you are far less likely to develop CTD- and RSI-related problems.

ERGONOMIC RULES TO FOLLOW WHEN USING YOUR COMPUTER

Arms

Arms should be hanging comfortably at your side and be bent at a 90-degree angle to your elbows.

Wrists

Wrists should be relaxed and in line with forearms.

Forearms

Forearms should be level with home row keys; if not, use a wrist rest. If you are using a keyboard or mouse often, swivel wrist supports that attach to your desk will make keying less stressful.

Monitor Your Monitor

Your monitor screen should be clean and free of smudges and positioned to be free of glare.

Adjust the brightness and contrast to a level that is comfortable for your eyes. (It will be easier on your eyes and neck if you place the monitor so that you look down at it.)

Your eyes should be 6–8 inches above the center of your screen, which should be 18–20 inches away.

Your monitor should not be on top of your CPU but at least a 10-degree angle downward.

The screen should be no more than a 40-degree angle from your straight-ahead position, and if you are using a source document, it should be the same distance away as the screen.

Feet

Your feet should be FLAT on the floor. If they do not reach the floor you will need a footrest.

Give Yourself a Break

Get up, take a break, and stretch every hour. I was not taking enough breaks until I installed stretching software. My stretching software consists of an animated figure that periodically comes up on my screen and begins to do exercises I can follow along with. If you don't want to get stretching software, keep a timer away from your desk (so you have to get up to turn it off) and set it to remind you when you need to take a break.

Don't Stress Your Eyes

Antiglare screens are highly recommended to reduce eye strain. If you wear glasses, you can also ask your optometrist for a special computer prescription. (It will save you strain in the long run.) If you don't want your vision to deteriorate, rest and move your eyes often. To do so, alternate from on to off screen tasks while you're working. Blinking three or four times also helps relax your eyes, as does focusing at far away distances when you take a break.

Posture

Sit upright with your shoulders back. Slouching puts undue pressure on your body.

How to Choose the Right Ergonomic Devices for You

There are many devices and different types of furniture available that all claim to be ergonomically designed, yet are all completely different. I urge you to take the time to learn about these devices. The more preventative precautions you take when using your computer, the better. A few of the right devices could save you from unnecessary pain and expensive trips to the doctor.

Workstations and Desks

Most furniture is made to accommodate a man up to six feet, two inches tall. Many small and petite men and women therefore need footrests so that their feet touch the floor. Inexpensive brands of workstations or computer tables may not have room for your legs or have a place for your monitor at a comfortable height. I spent days looking in computer furniture stores until I found a workstation that was best for my body size, as long as I added the right height footrest.

❓ Questions to Ask When You Buy a Workstation or Computer Desk

- Is the monitor shelf the right height for me?
- Is it adjustable?
- Does it block out glare on the screen?
- Does it have a built-in footrest?
- Does it have a built-in wrist rest?
- Does it come assembled?
- What is it made out of? (Not all fiberboards are the same—some scratch.)
- Are the fasteners strong enough? (Metal to metal is the strongest.)
- Does it have casters?
- Is it a space-saver design?
- Does it have a guarantee?
- Does it have a retractable mouse tray?
- Will my system fit in it? My printer? My peripherals?
- Does the keyboard shelf glide in and out?
- Do I like the way it looks?
- Is it comfortable?

Keyboard Draws and Arms

A regular desk is the correct height for writing, not for keyboarding. You may need to purchase a keyboard draw so that the keyboard is at the correct height for you. A keyboard draw is a drawer that attaches under your desk and is pulled out to hold your keyboard while you're using it. If you decide to buy one, make sure that it is the correct height so that your forearms are at a 90-

degree angle (or more) to your upper arms. Articulating keyboard platforms that have the ability to adjust the height and angles are a good idea if more than one person uses the computer.

Chairs

No matter what size you are, it is important to use a chair that is adjustable and allows your feet to touch the floor or footrest. Your body needs to be supported. If your back is not supported by the chair you use, you may need a backrest or roll.

[?] QUESTIONS TO ASK WHEN YOU BUY A CHAIR

- Can I adjust the seat and back angles?
- Does it have lumbar support?
- What kind of cushioning does it have?
- Is it guaranteed?

Wrist Rests

Wrist rests should not put any pressure on the bones in your wrist. The cushioning should offer support, but still be soft. They should be adjustable and washable.

[?] QUESTIONS TO ASK WHEN YOU BUY A WRIST REST

- Is it adjustable?
- Is the fabric washable? Does it absorb sweat? (Excess sweat can cause dermatitis.)
- How does it feel?
- Is there a companion rest for my mouse?

Arm Supports/Armrests

Studies have shown that stress on the neck, head, and shoulders while working on a keyboard can be significantly reduced with armrests. Arm supports are similar to an armrest on a chair, except that they connect directly to the keyboard table. Some models swivel with your arm movements and are adjustable. Others have a bouncy spring to them.

[?] QUESTIONS TO ASK WHEN YOU BUY ARM SUPPORTS

➤ In what ways are they adjustable?

➤ Do they swivel with the movement of my arms?

➤ What are they made out of?

➤ How do they feel?

➤ What is the philosophy behind the design?

Wrist Supports

Every where I go, I see workers wearing back support belts, and now I am beginning to see even the checkers at the market wear wrist supports or braces. I have tried several wrist supports. One model was made for both right and left hands, therefore the Velcro would catch on the fabric on my wrist rest. The fabric was too stiff to allow for the hand movement I needed. Finally, I found the WorkSmart wrist supports from Ergodyne. They are extremely well designed. They come in sizes for left or right hands. The fabric is stretchy and has an absorbent lining to absorb sweat. They are fully adjustable and have strong protective support on the underside. Many new wrist supports are coming out on the market. Therefore, we need to ask:

[?] QUESTIONS TO ASK WHEN YOU BUY WRIST SUPPORTS

➤ Do they come in different sizes for left and right hands?

➤ What are they made out of?

➤ Are they washable?

➤ Is there rough Velcro exposed that may catch on my clothes or wrist rest?

Backrests, Rolls, and Slings

Chairs are designed for an average-size person, but many of us are not average. You may need to supplement your chair with a support. There are various back supports of different shapes and sizes to help keep your body properly aligned, as well as slings that hold your back up with straps that go around your knees.

[?] QUESTIONS TO ASK WHEN YOU BUY BACKRESTS, ROLLS, AND SLINGS

➤ What is it made out of? Why?

➤ Is it washable?

➤ Is it adjustable?

➤ How does it attach to me or the chair?

Glare Screens

Glare screens make working on your monitor less stressful on your eyes. They also can shield out electromagnetic radiation. Your glare screen should be the right size for your monitor and be kept clean and free of smudges.

[?] QUESTIONS TO ASK WHEN YOU BUY A GLARE SCREEN

➤ What is it made out of?

➤ How do I clean it?

➤ How does it attach to my monitor?

➤ Does the screen scratch?

➤ Does it have an antistatic device?

➤ Does it meet the latest standards for blocking radiation?

Exercise Software

Doctor of Chiropractic Patrick St. John says, "The human body is not built to stay in the same position for long hours. It is important to move constantly, change the way you sit, stretch, and move back support pillows all day long." Dr. St. John's advice sounds easy to follow but when you're engrossed in your computer, you'll find that time warps and all of a sudden you'll realize that you've been working for ten hours without a break! That's why break or exercise software that stops you in the middle of your computer work is so important.

[?] QUESTIONS TO ASK WHEN YOU BUY EXERCISE/BREAK SOFTWARE

➤ Is it compatible with my operating system?

- Who designed the software and why?
- What kinds of exercises does it contain? Neck? Shoulder? Back? Legs? Eyes?
- Can I schedule regular breaks?
- Does it save my work?

Telephone Headsets

While talking on the phone, many people hold their shoulders to their ears. You don't need to be a chiropractor to know that this can cause pain. In my own business, now that I have a telephone headset, my phone life is much better. I can interview people on the phone and type at the same time. I also find that I am more comfortable while holding conversations, and my shear enthusiasm for my work comes through on the phone. I even can talk to long-winded friends without getting annoyed.

[?] QUESTIONS TO ASK WHEN YOU BUY A TELEPHONE HEADSET

- Is it FCC compliant?
- Is it compatible with my telephone?
- Does it have to be plugged into an electrical outlet?
- Does it have it's own dialer?
- Does it need batteries?
- Is the headset adjustable?

....

No one likes to live with pain—especially if it could have been prevented in the first place. Be sure to exercise caution and follow the ergonomic rules outlined in this chapter when setting up your work area. So be kind to yourself and do your exercises!

✍ CHAPTER 6 EXERCISES

1. Go to office supply stores, call for catalogues, and shop for the ergonomic furniture and equipment you need.
2. Adjust your furniture and equipment until you feel completely comfortable.
3. When you set up your work area, design it so that you will have to get up to answer the phone, go to the printer, get envelopes, etc. This may not save you time, but it will ensure that you keep moving.
4. Remember these ergonomic rules:
    a. When your body begins to feel tense, stop what you are doing immediately, stretch, and relax.
    b. Set up software or a timer (or an alarm clock) to remind you to take a break.
    c. Change the setup of your ergonomic devices to vary your body's position.
5. Photocopy the ergonomic rules from this book and post them where you work. Remember to take stretching breaks!
6. If you are experiencing any pain, see a professional immediately. Don't assume that the pain will go away by itself.

7 ✦ PLANNING YOUR BUSINESS

YOUR MAP TO SUCCESS

You would never expect to get to California from New York without a plan or a map, but many self-employed people expect to find their way to success without a business plan or even a compass. Your business plan is your road map to success. Having a plan doesn't mean that you won't take an alternate route once in a while, but it will make it easier to reach your desired destination of success and financial freedom.

Your business plan will lay out a work schedule and plot strategies to improve and increase business. You should figure out how much money you will need to start and run your business, and how much work you will have to put into it in order to make the money you want.

Expenses are purchases of items or services you need in order to run your business. You can not make a profit until you cover your expenses. For example, a friend of mine has a typing service and started out charging $15 an hour because that was what she made as a secretary. She did not figure the cost of her computer or paper, her billing time, the trips to the copy center and stationery store, her marketing costs, her self-employment tax, or her utilities and phone bill. When she sat down and figured out how much time she really worked, she was actually making less than $6 per hour. She was getting a lot of business because she was cheaper than everyone else, but she was completely unsatisfied. If she had figured all her time and expenses from the beginning, she could have avoided most of her problems.

One of the first things you need to do when setting up a business is to estimate your expenses. You will be surprised how quickly your phone bill goes up when you are calling 50 to 100 businesses a day. So be generous with your estimates.

MONTHLY EXPENSES

Since most bills are monthly, you can figure your expenses by the month.

$$ SOME COMMON MONTHLY EXPENSES:

Advertising

Car expenses

Cellular phone

Cleaning and repairs

Computer equipment

Copier & fax paper

Credit cards or interest

Freight charges

Insurance (be sure to insure your computer)

Maintenance

Messenger service

Office supplies

Office equipment

Transportation costs

Packing materials

Pagers

Publications/memberships /conferences

Rent

Self-employment tax

Shipping

Sick-pay fund

State and federal income tax

Stationery/envelopes

Tools

Training/consultants

Uniforms or dry cleaning

Utilities

Make a list of all your projected monthly expenses. Next to each item put an amount that is a little more than you expect that item to cost per month. Multiply your monthly expenses by 12 for your yearly expenses.

After you've figured the cost of your software and hardware, add training and whatever else you need to make up your start-up

■ PLANNING YOUR BUSINESS

costs. Many of your start-up costs can be deducted as expenses (check with your accountant, the IRS, or a good income tax book). Anyway you look at it, before you make a profit you will have to cover your expenses and start-up costs.

HOW MUCH TO CHARGE

After you estimate how much you want to make, here's a good way to estimate how much you need to charge per hour:

Take your desired yearly salary, divide it by 52, then divide the result by 40, then multiply that result by your expenses.

For instance, if you want to make $50,000 a year, divide $50,000 by 52. The result is $961.50 a week, which you divide by 40 to get $24.00 an hour. That's if you don't include your overhead and are working 40 hours a week.

If your overhead and monthly expenses are low, multiply your hourly rate by 2.1; if your overhead seems high, multiply it by 2.5. If you plan to charge by the hour, your hourly rate would be either $50.40 or $60.00. (Now do you see why professional service people like plumbers and car mechanics charge what they do?)

You will also want to find out what your competitors are charging. You can call and ask yourself, or have a friend check them out for you. If your competitors are all charging about the same rate, what could you do at the same rate that would impress your future clients?

FIGURING CLIENT NUMBERS & HOURS

After you figure out how much you need to charge, here's a good way to estimate how many client hours you will need to work a week:

Take the amount you want to make a year, add on your expenses, divide by how much you charge, then divide by 52.

For example, suppose you want to make $50,000 your first year and your start-up costs are $10,000 and your yearly expenses are $5,000—which all combine for a total of $65,000. If you want to charge $50 an hour, divide $65,000 by $50 to get 1,300. 1,300

81

divided by 52 is 25. Therefore, with this plan you will need to have 25 billable hours a week to make $50,000 per year.

Write down how many hours you need to work and then guesstimate how many clients you will need. (If you are starting part-time, reduce your yearly salary, and divide it by fewer hours.) Obviously, you will want clients who use as many hours of your services as possible, as opposed to clients who talk to you for hours and only pay you for an hour of work.

Be aware that when you start up, you will not have clients instantly and will need to spend more time marketing than actually working. It's a great idea to start handing out promotional materials even before your business is all set up and you're still at your old job. You can even check to see if your present employer may need you for freelance work.

📝 CHAPTER 7 EXERCISES

1. Using the information from this chapter, estimate your monthly and yearly expenses, salary, and hourly rate.
2. Call several competitors and ask what they charge and exactly what services they provide for that rate. Do their rates compare with what you want to make? If you want to charge more than they do, what additional services can you offer?
3. Call the IRS to get information on business taxes, or do your research through reference books.
4. Write up a price list for your services.
5. Set daily, weekly, and monthly goals for yourself. Can you see yourself meeting those goals? If not, set them at a more realistic level.
6. Think about what in your business might cause you problems. How can you avoid them? What are you not good at that you could hire someone else to do?
7. Research prices for expenses by calling local office supply stores and warehouses. Can you cut costs anywhere?
8. Is there anything else you think you need to do before you start marketing?
9. Map out a five-year plan for your business. Can you get in touch with someone who can help you figure out your business plan and costs? Where would you like to be in five years? How much would you like to be earning? Would you like to move? Have employees?

> ☑ *Checklist for Business Planning*
>
> ❑ Have you included every cost you can think of?
>
> ❑ Can you make your desired salary without killing yourself?
>
> ❑ Have you researched your business enough to know how long it will take until you make a profit?
>
> ❑ Will you be able to follow your plan? Is it set up in a logical manner and easy to follow?

8 ♦ MARKETING YOUR BUSINESS

TOOLS OF THE MARKETING TRADE

Marketing is the art of reaching potential clients, communicating who you are to them and why they should use your services. It is a very important ongoing process designed to generate interest in your services and is probably the most creative task you will be doing in your business. There are many ways to market your business and you have to decide what technique will best suit you, your business, and the clients you want to reach.

If you do not actively market your business, you may not be able to stay afloat your business. A student of mine once lamented, "I don't understand why I'm not making any money. I put one sign up at the car wash and I haven't gotten a single call." She didn't realize that she needed to take time to find the marketing tools that worked best for her business and not assume that one sign would do all the work her.

Marketing tools let potential clients know:

1. The features of your product or service.

2. What makes your service special.

3. How your service will benefit them.

To market your business successfully you will need to know:

1. Who your potential clients are.

2. What kinds of needs you will be fulfilling for them.

3. What tools will reach them best.

Make Money with Your PC!

WHAT MARKET ARE YOU TRYING TO REACH?

The clients you are trying to reach are your market. For instance, if you design wedding invitations and programs, your market would be brides and their families. They read bridal magazines, go to bridal shops and shows, and use the services of ministers, judges, and rabbis. If I was going to sell computerized make-over software for plastic surgeons which lets patients see what they will look like before they invest in plastic surgery, I would want to find the best way to reach plastic surgeons. Perhaps there is a plastic surgeon organization or a trade publication I could advertise in. I could buy lists of plastic surgeons and mail them my literature. I could look in the yellow pages and call every one of them up and invite them to a catered party where I will show my product. Or, I could call and offer them use of my product for a week free, to try it and see if their clients like it and if it increases the number of surgeries their patients want. I probably wouldn't put a sign up in a supermarket, but I might put up a tasteful flyer in the coffee shop of a medical building.

After you figure out what your market is, you can do market research to figure out what tools will reach it. Call businesses you think will be interested in your product and ask them if they ever need your services. You can also do your own survey and find out what type of person or business is most likely to need your service.

When I wanted to market my computer class, I realized that my clientele would be colleges and adult schools. I contacted every college and adult school in the area and sent them an intelligent letter, a course description, an outline, and a biography. Eventually, I booked my classes with over 75% of those contacted. My course description was so good they didn't have to write their own, and many printed it verbatim in their catalogues.

Use your imagination. Maybe there is a market out there that no one ever thought of before. In Los Angeles, there's fierce competition between desktop publishers and computer programmers, but I know two computer entrepreneurs who specialized in areas where there was little or no competition:

Suzanne, a nurse, turned her skill of conveying medical terms to patients in simple English into a profitable medical DTP business. She marketed her services to doctors who could save time explaining diseases and treatments by having a nice collection of her simple, friendly brochures about their treatments available to patients. The doctors were happy because they could save valuable time and the patients were happy because they could ask intelligent questions of the doctor.

Another successful entrepreneur, Krikor, is of Armenian ancestry. He can speak and write Armenian. When he saw that no one had a word processing program to print and write Armenian, he wrote a program that could and used his contacts through churches and Armenian organizations to make a nice profit from his work.

YOUR MARKETING TOOLS

Following are descriptions of various methods and tools which you can use to market your business. If you like a particular tool, research it further to see if it will work for you, or use it on a limited basis to test the response.

Advertising

Advertising comes in many forms. Simply put, you create an ad and buy space in a periodical, on a bench, or in some other medium. If you are going to write your own ad, remember to be creative. Be sure you have a memorable headline that draws the attention of the reader, and differentiate yourself from your competitors. Make sure that your ad is visually noticeable and easy to read.

On the other hand, if you are going to spend a lot of money in advertising, contact an advertising agency. These agencies' only purpose is to create ads; they make a profit by getting a percentage of the ad space their customers buy. If you decide to hire an agency, you will be spending a lot of time working with their staff. Therefore you will need to know what kind of questions to ask them.

❓ Questions to Ask if You Hire an Ad Agency

➤ Have you handled businesses like mine before?

➤ May I see some samples?

➤ What can you do for me?

➤ Who will be writing and designing my ad? Can I talk to them?

➤ Does the ad agency understand exactly what I want to do?

Advertising Gifts and Specialties

At a software demonstration, I was given a pen from a computer software company that works like a toy and is shaped like a pink Cadillac. The pen will go across an office floor in no time. Everyone who sees me use the pen laughs and wants to know where I got it. For the price of a pen, the company's name is being seen all over Los Angeles.

You can have a gift made with your name and phone number on it fairly cheaply that will reach many people. There are many items that can be imprinted, like scratch pads, rulers, key chains, calendars, T-shirts, caps, and shopping bags.

➤ What gift would best represent your business?

Articles in Publications

Since you are in a specialized business, you are an expert in your field and there is information that you know that other people will want to read about. Many local publications are dying for good material. Trade journals also need articles on the businesses they cover. You can call or write the editors with your ideas. If it is published, your article can be reproduced and distributed to prospective clients.

➤ What publication would you like to write for?

Associations and Club Memberships

The more people you know who know what you do and who you are, the better. Any association or club is a valuable source of clients and referrals (you can offer a special rate to members). Members trust you because they either know you or the people you associate with. To find associations in your area, look in the phone book or *The Encyclopedia of Associations* from Gale Research. You will be surprised at just how many clubs and associations exist.

➤ What kinds of organizations would you like to join?

Attire

Your clothes say who you are. If you dress as if you know what you are doing, people will believe it. I know it seems obvious, but I have heard of people going to job interviews in old worn-out jeans. Your dress should be appropriate to your business.

➤ How can you dress for success?

Audio Visual Aids

Audio visual aids, such as samples, charts, and multimedia tools, make you look good. People respond to many different senses. The more senses you reach them with, the more likely they will be interested in your service.

➤ What kind of audio visual aid would impress you? What kind would work the best for your business?

Balloons

A bakery opened near my house, and I never noticed it until they had placed a bunch of colorful balloons out in front. The sign was not ready in time but the balloons made me take a different look. Balloons can be imprinted with your name, have a catchy phrase on them, and be given to your clients' kids. Reaching people's children is an added plus in anyone's book.

➤ Would balloons make your business more noticeable?

Bulletin Boards

Bulletin boards are usually all over town—in markets, restaurants, libraries, parks, laundromats, health food stores—and are a great place to put up your cards and flyers for free! People do read them when they are looking for a service.

➤ What bulletins boards in your areas should have your business card or flyer?

Business Cards

Don't be too cheap when you have your cards made. People keep cards around for years. Make sure you have plenty of them on hand everywhere you go.

➤ What cards have you seen that you really liked and that left a lasting impression?

Caller-on-Hold Marketing

If you are fortunate enough to have telephone callers waiting to talk to you and they are on hold, why not have them listen to ads, music, and testimonials you have recorded? It will generate more interest in your business.

➤ What would you like to hear while you're on hold?

Classified Ads

Classified ads are available in many publications. Think about what classified publications you would look at if you wanted to find someone who does exactly what you do. Then call or write the publication you choose to find out the demographics of the publication so that you will have a good idea of the age, income, and interests of its circulation.

✎ **NOTE:** Some smart computer bizers have generated new clients by answering want ads with their own promotional materials instead of a resume.

Client Mailing List

Your clients are a valuable commodity. They know who you are and, if they are happy with what you do, they will recommend you to other people. Keep in touch with them and send them notes when you offer new services or newsletters. Also, be sure to keep backups of your lists of clients on paper and diskettes.

➤ What marketing tools can you combine with your client mailing list?

Cold Calling

Cold calling on the phone can save you hours of legwork. There have been times where I have called hundreds of businesses and through the calls found out who needed my services.

➤ Who can you call right now to see if they need your services?

Community Involvement

The more involved you are in your community, the more you will know what business opportunities exist within it. For instance, because you are part of the community, word of mouth may let you know about bids before the rest of the public, or that a new office building full of potential clients is opening.

➤ How could you get more involved in your community?

Consultations

If you give a free consultation, clients will be given the chance to check you out before they buy your services. They may also feel obligated to buy from you.

➤ What kind of free consultation could you offer to generate business?

Contests and Sweepstakes

Contests have done wonders for Publishers' Clearing House and Ed McMahon. There are federal and state rules governing them. Be sure to research first.

➤ What kind of contest would get your name out there?

Conventions or Trades Shows

People go to trade shows to find out about services. If you have wonderful brochures, great displays, and a great demonstration, people will want to purchase your services. It is also a wonderful way to build a mailing list. (I know one company that gets most of its business from the county fair.)

Trade shows and conventions are also an important way for you to meet people in your industry. At COMDEX (a computer industry trade show), one year I met an editor of *Compute* who called me two weeks later and assigned me an article to write. At the American Booksellers Association trade show, I met Oprah Winfrey and many other important media contacts.

➤ What trade shows or conventions would be great for your business?

Credit Policies

Credit policies may attract customers. If you are able to offer credit, or able to wait for your payment, you may get more business. Be careful and check out the credit applicant with a credit agency.

➤ What kind of credit policy would bring in more customers?

Customer Recourse Policy

If you offer a money-back guarantee or a warranty, you will attract more customers. Be sure that you can stand behind your guarantee.

➤ What kind of guarantee could you offer?

Customer Service

It costs five times more to attract a new customer than to keep an old one. Therefore, you've got to keep the customer satisfied. Find out what your customers want, give good service, always do the best job you can, and give people more than they expect.

➤ What could you do to inprove your customer service?

Days and Hours of Operation

When developing your market niche, your days and hours of operation make a difference. A college friend of mine ran a 24-hour copywriting service. She had more business than she knew what to do with it because people didn't decide until the last minute that they needed an ad or brochure written.

➤ Could changing your work hours increase your business?

Demonstrations

Show people what you can do and they will be impressed. You may be the fastest typist in the world but until someone sees you type 100 wpm they will not believe it.

➤ What kind of demonstration would sell you the best?

Direct-Mail Letters or Postcards

Direct mail is a very effective sales technique. Business people are very busy and don't have the time to go out looking for services. Therefore, if something comes in the mail from your business that impresses them, they will probably call you, rather than your competition.

You can buy mailing lists from mailing list brokers. There are also mailing services that will do the design, printing, and mailing of your ad. If you don't write well, hire a good writer. Be aware that the response rate is very low. You will have to send out quite a few. (Note: the response rate for direct mail increases considerably when it is followed up with a phone call.)

➤ What kind of direct mail do you respond to? What kind of direct mail would be best for your business?

Directory Listings

There are directories for everything imaginable and you can be listed in them for free. Be sure to get listed in as many as possible. To find out what kind of directories relate to your business, there is a directory of directories, *Directories in Print* published by Gale Research.

➤ What kind of directories could you be listed in?

Enthusiasm

The more joy and excitement you have about your service, the more joy and excitement your clients have about using your service. I have gotten clients because they liked my good sense of humor and the fact that whenever I answer the phone, I am extremely enthusiastic and that enthusiasm comes through in my voice. Enjoy your work and your clients will enjoy you.

➤ What are you doing in your business that needs enthusiasm?

Expert Files

Newspapers and periodicals frequently need to interview experts. To be a part of their expert file, all you have to do is write them and tell them what you are an expert in, and you may be quoted in a future article. Publicity expert Bob Stane had one client who was a financial analyst. He wrote the *Los Angeles Times* and asked to be put in their Expert File. He has been interviewed several times, appeared on the front page of the business section, and was given a $1000 raise because of it.

➤ What publications can you be an expert for?

Flyers

Flyers, like brochures, tell who you are. Yesterday, I picked up a flyer at the stationery store for an errand service. On it was a great photograph of two young, smiling college women. They looked like people I would like to hire. I saved the flyer.

➤ Where could you put flyers?

Friendly Follow-ups

Call your client and check on him/her. If your client has asked for information, get back to them, but don't waste their time. Keep your call friendly and show that you care.

➤ Who can you follow up on today?

Gift Certificates

Department stores have used gift certificates for years and so can

MARKETING YOUR BUSINESS

you. It takes no time to make a certificate on your computer, and your services may make a perfect gift.

➤ What kind of gift certificates could you offer?

Location

Where you are located is important to your clients.

➤ What are the advantages and selling points of your location?

Logos

Logos visually represent your identity. Symbols are easy to identify and enhance your image. Your logo should: be simple and clear, be harmonious with your name and make sense, be easy to identify, and be able to last a lifetime.

➤ How can you enhance your image with a logo?

Motto/Tagline

Your motto can help people remember you. A restaurant by my house was named "The Broken Drum." Its motto was a picture of a drum with a hole in it and a tagline which read, "You can't beat it." I will never forget their motto.

➤ What would be a great motto for you?

Newsletters

Newsletters are a wonderful marketing tool because they allow you to communicate directly with perspective clients. Clients often save the newsletters if they contain valuable information. A dentist once sent me a newsletter that I kept around for years because it had tips on how to maintain good dental health.

➤ How could a newsletter bring you business?

News Releases

News releases are special kinds of letters sent to the media which contain information about specific events. Anyone can send them. In fact, news releases are where a lot of papers and news services get their information. Bob Stane, who teaches a class called "How to Get Free Publicity," loves to tell the success stories of his students and their news releases. One of his students was interviewed for *Life* magazine, appeared on a radio talk show and a television show, was written about in the *Los Angeles Times* and other newspapers—all from the same news release!

➤ What news release can you write and send out this week?

Online Services

There are all sorts of forums and listings available on online services. I've heard of people who have met or been referred to new clients over online services. Others have used them to tap into databases of perspective clients.

➤ How could an online service help your business?

Order Forms/Invoices

Your order forms and invoices are reflections of your professionalism. Make sure that they are clear, concise, well designed, and well written.

➤ How could your forms look more professional?

Price

What you charge says a lot about who you are. I have heard many stories of people who were not hired as professionals because they charged too little! They were considered inexperienced because they did not know the going rate. Be certain that your rate is in line with other professionals.

➤ What do you want your prices to say about you?

Public Relations

Anytime your name appears in the media, in any form, it is free advertising. Personal appearances and interviews can generate interest in your company.

➤ How could you get your name in the media?

Radio & TV Commercials

In certain areas of the country, radio and TV advertising is not very expensive. Cable TV also offers low cost options. Research your area to see if it would be worth it for you.

➤ What TV and radio stations in your area are worth advertising on?

Reprints of Ads and Articles

Anytime you advertise or something is written about you in the media, make copies of it to send or hand out.

➤ What ads or articles can you reprint and send out?

Reputation

Maintain a good reputation at all costs. If you have a bad reputation, no matter how many marketing tools you use, you won't be successful. Be fair and avoid conflicts and court actions.

➤ What do you want your reputation to be?

Sales Training

There are sales courses everywhere that will teach you sales techniques and get you pumped up to go out and sell. If you are a lousy salesperson, enroll in a class today. You can also read books and magazines on the subject.

➤ What kind of sales training do you need?

Scripts

Write up and rehearse what you want to tell people about your business when you're on the phone and in public. The more you say what you want to say, the easier it will be for you to appear well-informed and articulate.

➤ What kind of script do you need to write for yourself?

Seminars, Lectures, and Speaking Events

Seminars and speaking events give you contact with potential clients. You can establish yourself as an expert and sell your wares at numerous clubs, colleges, and professional organizations. Be sure to get people to sign your mailing list.

➤ Where would you like to talk, speak, or lecture?

Signs

If there is no sign over your door or in your window, or on the building if you have a business address, get one. Many people may be passing by and don't even know you're there. You can also have small signs within your office, informing clients of specials and new services.

➤ What kind of sign would draw attention to your business?

Special Events/Publicity Stunts

Creating unusual, newsworthy events is an excellent way of getting your name in the media. Bill Zanker, founder of the Learning Annex, threw 10,000 one dollar bills off the top of the Empire State Building to say "New York, we love you," and was seen in all the media in New York.

More conventional events can include parties for your clients and grand openings for your business.

➤ What special events have you seen or been to, and never forgotten? What special event could you create?

Specialized Niche

If you are the only computer programmer in town who can program in Japanese, Lithuanian, and Yiddish, there is probably no one else who can compete with you, and clients will pay a premium for your services. When you find your niche, business will come very easily.

➤ What is your niche?

Take-One Boxes

Take-one boxes are usually found on countertops and are filled with free promotional literature. You can use them to display your brochures or flyers, and they can be placed in all sorts of interesting places. The coffee shop you frequent may love to put your flyers out.

➤ Where could you put a take-one box?

Telephone

Whether you are answering the phone or cold calling potential clients, your phone voice is an important sales tool. The phone is an excellent means of communication, so don't mumble or be unclear.

When you leave a message: state your name and phone number clearly; speak slowly and be articulate; ask for a return call to verify that your message was received; tell the person you're calling when they can reach you; and be friendly and polite.

When you record your outgoing message: give out any information that people call for frequently (address, fax number, hours of operation); ask for the caller's name, phone number, time to call back, and nature of their call; be friendly and inviting to new business; make it sound professional.

➤ How could you improve your telephone communications?

Testimonials

Testimonials are a very impressive tool for new clients. A few words by a prominent client written up in your brochure give you credibility and stature.

➤ Who can you ask for a testimonial?

Tie-ins with Other Businesses

Tie-ins are informal marketing methods which allow professionals to refer clients and business to each other. If you are a desktop publisher, maybe you could team up with a printer. Accountants work with attorneys. Professionals know that they need other professionals and are often willing to work with you. You will also want to have people whom you can refer your clients to. You could even share the cost of advertising and office space.

➤ Who or what kind of services could you ally with?

Toll-Free Phone Numbers

If your service covers a large area and much of your ordering is done on the phone, a toll-free number will increase your business. Check different phone companies to get the best rates.

➤ What could your toll-free number spell?

Yellow Page Listings and Ads

Don't miss the deadline, and be sure to be at the beginning of the listing. Be sure to proofread your ads carefully. Remember, you will be paying for your listing on your phone bill and if for any reason you cannot pay your phone bill, you may lose your phone number, which is business suicide.

➤ Where should you be listed in your phone directory?

CHOOSING YOUR TOOLS

Some marketing methods and tools are more expensive than others. One may jump out at you from the list, or you may think of your own. Write down the ones that you think you could use best in your business. You could combine any or all of the above.

Since there are so many advertising strategies, think about why you remember the ads you do. Did you need to see them several times? Are they clever or unusual? Or, are they done in just plain good taste?

What exercises would you make up for this chapter? You know they're coming. Add yours to the end of mine.

✍ CHAPTER 8 EXERCISES

1. Collect your favorite ads, brochures, specialty items, or marketing tools you have seen from other businesses. What makes them memorable? What have you learned from them?
2. Choose five tools and research how to implement them.
3. Answer these questions and then decide what tools would illustrate them best.
    a. What is the objective of your marketing?
    b. What is special or unique about your service?
    c. What are the most important features/functions of your business?
    d. What problems can you solve for your client and how do you do it?
    e. What are the benefits of your service to your clients?
    f. What are the features of your service?
    g. What is your competition and how are you better or worse?
4. Write an ad for your business. Show it to everyone you know to see what they think.
5. Now write out a marketing plan for the coming year.
    Include in it:
    a. Tools you will use every day and goals for the tools. For example, you will call twenty people a day and mail out at least five flyers a week.
    b. Estimated cost.
    c. Weekly and monthly goals.

9 ♦ MANAGING YOUR BUSINESS

Managing It All

Managing your business requires good record keeping, good use of your time, and constant reevaluation of goals and priorities. To manage a successful computer-based business, you will have to carefully handle and control every aspect of the business: money, information, records, time, and maybe even personnel. In order to do this, you will need to develop systems to keep track of everything—and to keep your cool. Remember, although keeping records may be tedious, it will pay off for you in increased business and knowledge.

MONEY MANAGEMENT

The only way to know if you are making a profit is by keeping track of how much money goes out and how much money comes in. Earlier I mentioned quite a few simple accounting programs which are great because you don't need to be a CPA to understand them. If you don't buy an accounting program, read up on the subject in the library or through IRS publications. Money records are important not only because they tell you what is going on with your business; they can also be interpreted to help you make financial decisions for the future. One prominent Beverly Hills tax attorney suggests, "Keep records of everything and never throw them away."

When you first start out, you will want to try to collect your receivables as fast as possible to keep a healthy cash flow.

To be ready for the IRS, keep track of:

Credit card slips and receipts for cash

Documentation for expenses and correspondence

Your business mileage

Billing and invoicing

Inventory

Sales

Organize and record your receipts frequently throughout the month to avoid doing it all at once and losing information. (This will also help you with your estimated taxes.)

What Can You Deduct?

Deductions are expenses that are ordinary and necessary in the trade or business that you are in which facilitate and help to carry out functions of business.

TYPICAL TAX EXPENSES

Accounting services

Advertising

Automobile mileage, repair, maintenance, depreciation

Bad debt

Books and periodicals related to your business

Business travel

Club and professional association dues

Education expenses for improving and maintaining skills

Freight charges

Furniture and equipment

Insurance

Interest

Licenses

Maintenance

Office expenses and supplies

Postage

Printing and copying

Professional consultants' and attorneys' fees

■ MANAGING YOUR BUSINESS

Publicity

Rent (or office use of your home).

Salaries

Sales commissions

Utilities

TAX WARNING! ....
Like computer equipment, tax laws change all the time, so you'll need to keep up to date with new laws and with new IRS publications. The normal statute of limitations for tax returns is three years. If you fail to report over 25% of your gross income, the limit is six years. If your return is fraudulent or if you don't file a return, there is no statute of limitations and the IRS can go after you indefinitely.

GETTING ORGANIZED

If you throw all your papers on your desk and just let them pile up, how easy is it to find something when you need it? Maybe I should say, how hard is it to find something when you need it? File cabinets were invented for a reason and a good filing system will save you a lot of time and aggravation. The same is true of your computer files. Make folders and directories on your hard disk so that you know where to find something when you need it.

There are numerous methods to get organized: you can set up different binders or folders for different clients; set up databases; or keep everything in your daily planner.

Some wonderful tools to manage information are:

1. Database programs

2. Calendar and planning systems such as Day-Timers

3. Ready-made forms such as phone logs

4. Palm top computers

5. Calendar and planner software

When you keep your records, be sure to:

1. Record names, phone numbers, and dates of contact with clients.

2. Have a method of organizing all your information that makes sense not only to you, but also to your accountant and employees.

3. Keep a backup or extra copy of all your records (even phone books).

4. Backup! BACKUP! BACKUP! Backup new data every night!

☞ REMINDER: BACKUP!

I know this subject has been mentioned before, but if you don't make backup copies of your work, and something happens to your systems the loss will be tremendous. In fact, according to IDC, recovering lost data can take as long as 42 days and cost as much as $96,000. Only 6% of businesses survive more than two years after a major loss of data!

✔ CHECK FOR VIRUSES

If you're messing around with software and you don't know where it is from, make sure you give it a virus test.

TIME MANAGEMENT

Your time is valuable and how you use it determines how much money you make. How many times have you wished that you planned or scheduled your day better? Planning ahead is very important, as is estimating how long it takes you to get things done. The best way to manage your time is to make "To Do" lists and prioritize your activities. You'll be amazed at how fast you can get things done if you know what you have to do, and in what order you have to do them.

Time Management Hints:

- Look at the way you do things and figure out if there are better and more efficient ways.

- Keep a list of short jobs to do when things slow down. This way you can keep everything in order.

- Set up a workday ritual and schedule. We are creatures of habit. Get into the habit of working every day.
- Keep trade journals handy and read them when you have time.
- Say no to friends who think because you are in business for yourself you don't have to work during the day.

PERSONNEL MANAGEMENT

People respond to being treated with kindness and respect. When you become successful enough to hire others, never forget what it is like to work for someone else. Your employees' productivity will increase when they are happy and treated well.

BIDDING, BILLING, AND GETTING PAID

In my classes, I have heard numerous horror stories of clients not paying for services rendered. One student continued to work for a client even though the client owed him several thousand dollars. The client went bankrupt and the student never got his money. Last year, I had to take two clients to small claims court and, even though I did eventually get my money, it wasted a lot of time.

When working with a new client, get a deposit and as much money up front as possible. There is nothing wrong with asking for a deposit and checking to make sure that your client can afford to pay for your services. It could save you time in court and collection fees. Do not hand over completed assignments until the client has paid in full. After you have worked with the client, you can extend credit.

Warning Signs That You May Not Get Paid

1. They refuse to give you a deposit.
2. They refuse to give you credit references.
3. They refuse to sign a payment agreement or memo.
4. You have a gut feeling that they won't pay.

NOTE: If you have any doubt at all about accepting a check from a new client, you can call their bank and check for sufficient funds, and then make sure to cash the check immediately. Banks also offer check guarantee services for a fee.

When you bill, your bills should:

1. Be clear and simple.
2. Include a self-addressed stamped envelope.
3. Include documentation.
4. State clearly the terms and when it is due.
5. Avoid the word "due" and use the words "please pay."
6. State clearly if there is a late penalty or interest.

When a bill is late, call or send a letter immediately and keep a record or copy—just in case you need it in court.

BIDDING

When you're involved in bidding, your life will be much easier if you ask a lot of questions in the beginning. For instance, if you ask up front, "How much are you paying now?" at least you will have a starting point to begin from.

Your bid should:

Be specific and include anything that the client may misunderstand.

Show what the client will be charged for and how much.

State terms of payment.

Be clear about rates for changes in the original agreement.

If your initial bid is too low, believe me, you will regret it. Always have some way of renegotiating if the client changes what was originally asked for.

📖 Managing Your Business

☞ REMINDER

Management is the art of taking in information from many sources and making decisions based on your knowledge of that information. Like any other art it requires practice. You will need to exercise your skills. Start by completing the following exercises.

✍ CHAPTER 9 EXERCISES

1. What kind of bookkeeping and accounting do you want to set up? How do you want to do it? With books or on your computer?

2. What questions do you have about your tax liabilities? Call your accountant, or call or write the IRS to get answers.

3. What methods can you create to keep track of all the information you need?

    a. What kind of information do you want to be sure to keep track of?

    b. Map out a plan setting up a certain day or time to organize and file records.

4. How are you currently wasting a lot of time?

    a. What can you do to manage your time better?

5. Find a calendar system like Day-Timers, buy it and start using it immediately.

6. Set up and design a bid form and an invoice form; be sure to include the necessary information.

7. Make up management rules for your business and try them out.

8. Decide how you are going to backup your data.

10 ♦ LET'S GET BUSY!

MAKING THE TRANSITION

Congratulations! After reading all of the chapters and doing all of the exercises, you now know more than most people do when they start their computer-based business. You are prepared. Let's review your plan of action:

1. You have researched and decided what computer business best suits your skills and talents.
2. You have purchased your computer and software and have learned how to use it all.
3. You have researched your business, its competitors, and your market.
4. You have picked a name for your business that is memorable and that represents what you are planning to accomplish.
5. You have a great location that will benefit your business and have contacted your city, county, and state for licenses, variances, and tax information.
6. You have drawn up an easy-to-follow business plan, plotting your expenses, and you know how much money you need to bring in to cover your expenses.
7. You have set up an accounting system and an information system and designed your invoices.
8. You have developed a marketing plan suited to your business which is creative, well developed, and flexible.
9. You have designed and planned a daily work routine.

10. You have knock-'em-dead samples of your work.
11. You have excellent business cards, stationery, and a great brochure.
12. You have made the deadline for your phone book listing if you are getting a business phone.
13. You have set up a workplace for comfort and efficiency.
14. You have purchased the office supplies that you'll need.

There are a few more things you may want to do before you start working at your own business full-time:

1. Make sure it is really what you want to do.
2. Discuss your plans with your family and spouse.
3. Save enough money to cover several months' expenses.
4. Join support groups that will help you through your transition.
5. Attend industry conventions, organizations, and trade shows.

When you first start working you will face many challenges, but there are many places you can go for help. Professional trade organizations, the Small Business Administration, and SCORE are more than willing to help. Magazines like *Home Office Computing* have excellent articles on how to run and market your business.

TIME SAVERS, MONEY MAKERS, AND GOOD IDEAS

Time is money. The more time you save, the more money you make. Here are some good time savers and good ideas:

- Always ask as many questions as possible.
- Shop for services you use often.
- Sell your computer time when you're not using it.
- Hire a typist who is cheaper and better than you are.
- Hire a subcontractor if you don't have time to do all the work yourself.

Let's Get Busy!

- Print double-sided when mailing a long document.
- If you work from you home and have a business phone, only take incoming calls on it. Dial out on your personal phone for lower rates.
- Save phone charges by sending faxes late at night and very early in the morning.
- Save unnecessary trips to the post office by buying stamps in various denominations and a postage scale. Let your letter carrier pick up your outgoing mail when he/she delivers your mail.
- Charge a markup for expenses, messengers, faxes, color output, and long travel distances.
- Charge extra for rush jobs, weekends, and holidays.
- Charge for output from laser printers, especially on large jobs.
- Charge extra for copy/text in handwritten scribbles.
- Charge for revisions past a maximum allowed number of changes.
- Shut off your laser printer when you are not using it.
- Invoice on a regular basis.
- Whenever you hear of a great idea, write it down and remember to use it.

Now what? Follow your plan and you will succeed. If you have questions about your business, as you know by now, all you have to do is ask and you will find the answers.

Starting your own computer-based business is an exciting process, an adventure with great rewards. You are a part of a new breed of pioneers crossing the plains of outmoded methods of work to a new frontier of happiness, freedom, and success. Now, you have the talent, the knowledge, and supplies to get where you're going!

✍ CREATE YOUR OWN EXERCISES

What are your exercises? From now on, it's up to you. If you continue to read about and research your business, you will always have new ideas and be able to keep your business successful. I hope I have given the information and ideas you need, and wish you great luck and success in expanding on what you have learned in *Make Money with Your PC!* I trust that you will create better, more exciting and profitable computer-based businesses than I ever dreamed possible. Let's get busy! Get to work! Happy computing!

Resource Guide

ASSOCIATIONS

American Women's Economic Development Corporation, (800) 222-AWED—Nonprofit agency that helps women who are starting a business or who are already in business.

National Association of Desktop Publishers, (800) 874-4113—Largest trade association for desktop publishers in the country.

National Federation of Independent Business, (800) 634-2669—Publishes an excellent magazine for members and lobbies for laws that foster business.

Service Core of Retired Executives (SCORE), (800) 827-5722—Free advice from retired professionals. Check your library or phone book for local offices.

Small Business Administration, (800) 827-5722—Check your library or phone book for local offices.

BOOKS

Business Books

Blum, Laurie. *Free Money for Small Businesses and Entrepreneurs.* John Wiley & Sons Inc., 1988.

Alarid, William M. and Gustav Berle. *Free Help from Uncle Sam to Start Your Own Business.* Puma Publishing Co., 1992.

Frost, Ted S. *The Second Coming of the Wooly Mammoth.* Ten Speed Press, 1991.

Hodge, Cecil C., Sr., *Mail Order Moonlighting (Revised Edition).* Ten Speed Press, 1988.

Holland, Phillip. *How to Start a Business Without Quitting Your Job.* Ten Speed Press, 1992.

Ingram, Colin. *The Small Business Test*. Ten Speed Press, 1990.

J.K. Lasser Institute. *J.K. Lasser's Your Income Tax*. Prentice Hall, 1994.

Kamaroff, Bernard. *Small Time Operator*. Bells Springs Pub., 1994.

Pring, Roger. *The Instant Business Forms Book*. John Wiley & Sons, 1987.

Schepp, Brad. *The Telecommuter's Handbook*. Pharos Books, 1990.

Shenson, Howard L. *The Contract and Fee Setting Guide for Consultants and Professionals*. John Wiley & Sons, 1990.

Whitmyer, Claude, Salli Rasberry, and Michael Phillips. *Running a One Person Business*. Ten Speed Press, 1989.

Career Decision Books

Bolles, Richard Nelson. *What Color Is Your Parachute?* Ten Speed Press, 1994.

Chaney, Marti with Vicki Thayer. *Imagine Loving Your Work*. Celestial Arts, 1993.

Desktop Publishing Books

Kramer, Felix and Maggie Lovass. *Desktop Publishing Success: How to Start and Run a Desktop Publishing Business*. Business One Irwin, 1991.

Ergonomic Books

Gach, Michael Reed. *The Bum Back Book*. Celestial Arts, 1983.

Sellers, Don. *ZAP! How Your Computer Can Hurt You and What You Can Do About It*. Peachpit Press, 1994.

Sussman, Martin and Dr. Ernest Lowenstein, with Howard Sann. *Total Health at the Computer*. Station Hill Press, 1993.

Marketing Books

Bly, Robert W. *The Copywriter's Handbook*. Henry Holt & Co., 1985.

Bly, Robert W. *Selling Your Services*. Henry Holt & Company, 1991.

Levine, Michael. *Guerilla P.R.: Waging an Effective Publicity Campaign Without Growing Broke*. Harper Business, 1993.

Levinson, Jay Conrad. *Guerilla Marketing Attack*. Houghton Mifflin Company, 1989.

Money & Personal Empowerment Books

(The following money and personal empowerment books are available through LuminEssence Productions, P.O. Box 19117, Oakland, CA 94619.)

Roman, Sanaya and Duane Packer. *Creating Money*. H.J. Kramer Inc., 1988.

Roman, Sanaya. *Living with Joy*. H.J. Kramer Inc., 1986.

Roman, Sanaya. *Personal Power Through Awareness*. H.J. Kramer Inc., 1986.

Computer Books

Bear, John, Ph.D. *Computer Wimp No More*. Ten Speed Press, 1992.

Magid, Lawrence J. *The Little PC Book*. Peachpit Press, 1993.

Naiman, Arthur, Nancy E. Dunn, Susan McCallister, John Kadyk, et al. *The Macintosh Bible*. Peachpit Press, 1993.

Reference Books

Directories in Print. Gale Research International.

The Software Encyclopedia, R.R. Bowker.

MAGAZINES

Home Office Computing, (800) 288-7812, P.O. Box 51344, Boulder, CO 80321-1344.

Inc., (800) 234-0999, P.O. Box 51534, Boulder, CO 80321-1534.

Income Opportunities, P.O. Box 55206, Boulder, CO 80322.

Info World, (708) 647-7925, P.O. Box 1172, Skokie, IL 60076-8153.

MacUser, (800) 627-2247, P.O. Box 56986, Boulder, CO 80321.

Macworld, (800) 288-6848, P.O. Box 4529, Boulder, CO 80322.

PC Computing, (800) 365-2770, P.O. Box 58229, Boulder, CO 80322-8229.

PC Magazine, (800) 289-0429, P.O. Box 51524, Boulder, CO 80321-1524.

PC Novice, (800) 241-6600, P.O. Box 85380, Lincoln, NE 68501-9877.

PC World, (800) 234-3498, P.O. Box 5029, Boulder, CO 80322-5029.

Publish, (800) 685-3435, P.O. Box 5039, Brentwood, TN 37024.

The Macintosh Product Registry, (407) 231-6904, Redgate Communications Corp., 660 Beachland Blvd., Vero Beach, FL 32963.

Windows Magazine, (800) 829-9150, P.O. Box 420235, Palm Coast, Fl 32142-0235.

Windows Sources, (800) 365-3414, P.O. Box 51900, Boulder, CO 80322-1900.

NEWSPAPERS

(Note: there may be similar newspapers in your area. Look for them at your local computer store and/or library.)

Computer Currents, (800) 365-7773, 5720 Hollis Street, Emeryville, CA 94608.

The Computer Post, (204) 947-9766, 301-68 Higgins Ave., Winnipeg MB R3B OA5 Canada.

Computer User, (612) 339-7571, MSP Communications, 220 South 6th Street, Ste. 500, Minneapolis, MN 55402.

Micro Publishing News, (310) 371-5787, 21150 Hawthorne Blvd. #104, Torrance, CA 90503.

Micro Times, (510) 934-3700, Bam Publications, 3470 Buskirk Ave., Pleasant Hill, CA 94523.

ONLINE SERVICES/BULLETIN BOARDS

America Online, (800) 827-6364.

CompuServe, (800) 368-3343.

Prodigy, (800) PRODIGY.

USER GROUPS

User Group Locator Line, (914) 876-6678.

Apple Information, (800) 538-9696.

COMPUTER BUSINESS & COMPUTER CONSULTANT

Lynn Walford, c/o Ten Speed Press, P.O. Box 7123, Berkeley, CA 94707. I am available for lectures, seminars, radio and TV appearances/interviews, and private consultations. Please write me and tell me if you have any wonderful sources for your fellow computer-based business owners and they may appear in the next edition of this book. I love success stories.

COMPUTER DIRECT DEALERS

(For a dealer in your area contact Computing Technology Industry Association, (708) 268-1818. For an Apple dealer contact (800) 538-9696.)

Central Technology, (310) 828-0047.

Compaq, (800) 888-6139.

Comtrade, (800) 969-2123.

Dell Computer, (800) 289-3355.

Gateway 2000, (800) 846-2000.

IBM, (800) 772-2227.

Insight, (800) 927-7848.

Micron, (800) 438-3343.

Quill Corporation, (708) 634-6650.

Zeos, (800) 423-5891.

SUPPLIERS/MAKERS OF COMPUTER ERGONOMIC FURNITURE, DEVICES, AND SOFTWARE

Ergodyne, (800) 225-8238—Intelligently designed wrist rests, wrist supports, footrests, back supports, and stretch software.

Kantek, (800) 536-3212—Glare screens that eliminate static and radiation.

Kinesis Corporation, (206) 455-9220—Innovative ergonomic keyboards.

MicroCentre, (800) 966-5511—Quality workstations with great, comforting ergonomic features.

Make Money with Your PC!

Nada-Chair, (800) 722-2587—Back slings that support you when your chair doesn't.

Quill Corporation, (708) 634-4800—Many ergonomic products not available anywhere else. Quill has an ergonomic specialist on staff to help you choose products to fit your needs.

COMPUTER INSURANCE

The Computer Insurance Agency, (800) 722-0385.

SAFEWARE, (800) 848-3469.

RESOURCES FOR THE DISABLED

Don Johnston Inc., (800) 999-4660—Catalogue of computer hardware and software for people with special needs.

HumanWare Inc., (800) 722-3393—Computer products for the visually impaired.

IBM Independence Series Center, (800) 426-4832—Catalogue and direct sale of IBM products for the disabled.

NARIC (National Rehabilitation Information Center) and ABLE DATA, (800) 227-0216—Library and information center that offers free brochures and referrals for resources and products for the disabled.

Trace Research and Development Center, (608) 262-6966—Maintains a database and publishes a catalogue of assistant techonology.

WCIL (Westside Center for Independent Living), (310) 390-3611—Nonprofit agency that helps the disabled in many ways, including computer training, political advocacy, and housing.